CLEAN EATING MEAL PREP

Clean Eating

MEAL PREP

6 Weekly Plans and 75 Recipes
for Ready-to-Go Meals

Emily Kyle, MS, RDN, HCP, and Phil Kyle, Chef

Photography by Darren Muir

ROCKRIDGE
PRESS

This book is dedicated to you, so that you can live your life to the fullest in the best health possible.

For general information on our other products and services or to obtain technical support, please contact our Customer Care Department within the United States at (866) 744-2665, or outside the United States at (510) 253-0500.

Rockridge Press publishes its books in a variety of electronic and print formats. Some content that appears in print may not be available in electronic books, and vice versa.

TRADEMARKS: Rockridge Press and the Rockridge Press logo are trademarks or registered trademarks of Callisto Media Inc. and/or its affiliates, in the United States and other countries, and may not be used without written permission. All other trademarks are the property of their respective owners. Rockridge Press is not associated with any product or vendor mentioned in this book.

Interior and Cover Designer: Emma Hall
Art Producer: Sara Feinstein
Editor: Claire Yee
Production Editor: Ruth Sakata Corley

Photography © 2020 Darren Muir. Food styling by Yolanda Muir. Author photo courtesy of Cassi V Photography.

ISBN: Print 978-1-64739-745-6
eBook 978-1-64739-447-9

R0

Contents

Introduction

Hello, there! Today is the first day of your new clean-eating meal-prepping lifestyle and we couldn't be more excited that you've chosen us to help guide your journey!

My name is Emily Kyle, and I am a Registered Dietitian Nutritionist and certified Holistic Cannabis Practitioner who has spent the last five years helping people just like you live happier, healthier lives. I am proud to pair my expertise as a dietitian with the expertise of my creative and talented husband, Phil Kyle ("Chef Phil"). Although Phil prefers to be the man behind the curtain, he has been here every step of the way, helping me turn all my nutrition knowledge into recipes that taste great, too.

I was given all the fundamental knowledge of nutrient density, macronutrient metabolism, and human physiology in my quest to become a dietitian, but as time went on, I found it was difficult to practice what I preached. As a busy mom with a growing business and a five-year-old to care for, I found myself taking shortcuts—choosing coffee over real food for breakfast; skipping lunch to work an extra hour, and overeating at dinner because I hadn't eaten properly during the day.

After feeling exhausted and burned-out for too long, I realized I wasn't fueling my body properly to feel my best. I recognized it was time for me to practice what I preached and put a concentrated effort toward planning and preparing meals with nourishing ingredients so I could keep up with my son, our small farm, and my growing business. Step one was getting back to basics by focusing on real, whole foods. Step two was committing to the plan by dedicating my time to meal-prepping those nourishing foods once a week.

So, if you're here with me today feeling chronically exhausted, undernourished, and strapped for time and wondering if making a switch to the clean-eating meal-prepping lifestyle works, let me tell you it does. It's worked for my clients and it's worked for me. Meal prepping can help you stay committed to clean eating by ensuring you are always prepared with healthy meals on hand. And although meal prepping may seem like a time investment at first, you'll soon come to love its convenience and will quickly learn how to pair the process with the slow-down-and-savor philosophy of clean eating.

From one human to another, trust me, I get it. Life is crazy busy and it can be tempting to make less-than-nourishing food choices when you're constantly on the go. But, ultimately, we all want more for our lives than to feel tired and burned-out all the time. This book will help you get there, and I hope it becomes a valuable tool to make eating clean simpler to do amid the everyday demands of life.

PART ONE

Clean Eating and Meal Prep: A Perfect Pairing

Welcome to clean eating! Part 1 of this book introduces you to the clean-eating meal-prepping lifestyle—a simple way of life that values whole plant-based foods, nourishment over convenience, and joyful movement to help you feel your best. To make this new lifestyle transition as easy as possible, we'll focus on teaching you how to prepare clean-eating meals to ensure you're able to reach your goals as effortlessly as possible.

Crunchy Kale Salad, page 71

CHAPTER ONE

The Clean-Eating Lifestyle

A clean-eating lifestyle is not a short-term diet that exclusively restricts any one food or food group. Rather, clean eating is all about living a life dedicated to the belief that whole, natural foods nourish the body and offer sustainable long-term health benefits. A clean-eating lifestyle can be adapted easily to fit individual dietary and cultural needs. At its core, clean eating is meant to be accessible and enjoyable for all.

This first chapter gives you everything you need to know about clean eating. Chapter 2 dives into why meal prepping is the perfect way for you to start and maintain your clean-eating lifestyle long term. When paired together, clean eating and meal prepping will benefit both your physical and mental health, allowing you to reduce anxiety and stress in the kitchen and, ultimately, giving you more time to enjoy food with the ones you love.

What Does It Mean to Eat Clean?

A traditional clean-eating lifestyle is based on the four tenets of clean eating:

1. Eating real food

2. Maximizing plant-based foods in your diet

3. Valuing nourishment over convenience

4. Finding enjoyable ways to stay active

The beauty of clean eating is you can personalize it to fit your needs. Ultimately, this lets you create long-lasting positive change to support your health.

The core of clean eating lies in the first tenet: eating real food. Whole real foods are the most important foundation of the clean-eating lifestyle. "Real foods" are single-ingredient foods in their most natural state. For example, a whole apple, a broccoli stalk, a cut of beef, and whole-grain brown rice. These are all single-ingredient, nutrient-dense, whole, real foods that have not undergone extensive processing.

The second tenet of clean eating is maximizing consumption of plant-based foods. Although there is room for high-quality animal products within the clean-eating lifestyle, there is no debate that the single greatest source of health benefits comes from plant-based foods, including fruits, vegetables, beans and legumes, nuts, seeds, and fungi.

The third tenet puts the first two tenets into action by stressing the value of nourishment over convenience. Part of the clean-eating lifestyle involves making a personal commitment to value yourself and your health goals, even if it takes time. This is where meal prep comes in, to make clean eating accessible and stress-free. A few hours of concentrated effort per week will keep you on track and you'll get used to the process sooner than you might think.

The final tenet of the clean-eating lifestyle is finding physical activity through joyful movement. You don't need to hit the gym five times a week (unless you want to!), just find a physical activity you *love enough* to do at least three times weekly. Whether it's walking around your neighborhood with your kids after dinner, yoga class, or weekend hiking with friends, the activity you choose should be something you enjoy.

CLEAN-EATING STAPLES

The following items are clean-eating staples you should always have on hand:

Beans and Legumes: Whether canned or dried, beans and legumes are power-houses of complex carbohydrates, dietary fiber, and plant-based protein.

Beverages: Clean eating means clean drinking, too. Stock up on sugar-free, low-calorie options such as water, tea, coconut milk, or homemade nut milk.

Dairy: Clean eating can involve a portion of high-quality dairy products, as long as you are mindful of your personal tolerance for dairy (everyone's is different!).

Fats and Oils: Healthy dietary fats play an important role in good health. Limited animal products, full-fat dairy products, and plant-based options such as whole avocados, avocado oil, coconut oil, and olive oil are important staples.

Fish and Seafood: Wild-caught fish and seafood provide protein, omega-3 fatty acids, vitamins, and minerals. Wild-caught seafood tends to contain less saturated fat than farmed varieties. Fresh, canned, and frozen options can all fit into a clean-eating lifestyle and are great for meal prep.

Fruit and Berries: Fruit is an important dietary source of vitamins, minerals, and antioxidants and serves as a natural sweetener in many recipes. When fresh fruits aren't available, frozen fruits can provide the same nutrition.

Herbs and Spices: Herbs and spices provide flavor, vitamins, and minerals. They are also a particularly good source of antioxidants. Stock up on fresh or dried herbs and spices that contain no preservatives, additives, or artificial ingredients.

Nuts and Seeds: Nuts and seeds, along with nut and seed butters, provide heart-healthy fats and other vitamins and minerals.

Protein: Clean eating is accessible to omnivores and vegetarians alike—whether you consume animal- or plant-based protein (or both) is your choice. Whatever you choose, look for organic options whenever possible.

Vegetables: In all forms—including fresh, frozen, and canned—vegetables play an important role in a clean-eating lifestyle. Focus on consuming a wide variety of colorful, cruciferous, and root vegetables, along with dark leafy greens and lettuce.

Whole Grains: Whole grains (both glutinous and gluten-free options) are an important source of dietary fiber, B vitamins, and antioxidants. Grains such as brown rice and quinoa are easy to cook ahead for meal-prep purposes.

Selecting Ingredients and Shopping in Season

You can shop for real whole foods at your local grocery store or your favorite farmers' market, or you can even grow them in your backyard. We recommend finding somewhere to shop that you love—a place where you are comfortable spending time and can truly enjoy the meal-prep process.

Whether you shop at a grocery store or a farmers' market depends largely on availability. Farmers' markets offer high-quality, often organic, and more affordable produce but they are not always accessible. Farmers' market products also vary from week to week and season to season. For this reason, we recommend shopping first at your local farmers' market, then a local grocery store for anything you couldn't find at the market.

When shopping for produce, carefully check for ripeness and freshness. Don't choose anything that is close to overripe (or extremely underripe). Avoid produce that is mushy, blemished, or looks like it will spoil soon. If you can't find a fresh option, select a frozen version or something similar. Use the ingredient swaps in the following table to help:

SEASON(S)	INGREDIENT CALLED FOR	SEASONAL SWAP
Winter	Fresh fruit, berries	Frozen fruit, berries
Early spring	Fresh broccoli, cauliflower	Frozen broccoli, cauliflower
Summer	Winter squash	Yellow squash, zucchini
Fall/Early winter	Plums, peaches, stone fruit	Pears

Beyond Your Plate

The clean-eating lifestyle is just that: a lifestyle. It's more than just the food you eat and the exercise you do—it encompasses your relationship to food, how you feel about your physical activity, and everything in between. It's a far cry from short-term diets, which can often be extreme with results that don't last. The clean-eating lifestyle builds upon simple, daily habits you enjoy so you can naturally create a sustainable practice that works for you, not against you.

Second only to enjoyment, frequency and consistency are the most important elements of physical activity. It may take you a few weeks to find the physical activity that works best for you, and that's okay. While you take the time to explore the many different physical activity options available, we will keep you nourished with delicious post-workout options, like the Creamy Cocoa-Mint Smoothie (page 96). Prep the snacks and treats in chapter 6 (page 81) to keep you fueled and ready to go for your favorite workouts.

CHAPTER TWO

The Fundamentals of Meal Prep

Before you get busy in the kitchen, we'll help you set yourself up for success by sharing a few of our favorite tips and tricks. Starting with this base of knowledge will make it easier for you to execute and sustain this lifestyle long term.

The concept of meal prepping is simple: Commit a few hours on a day you choose to prepare meals for the week. This 2- or 3-hour time commitment typically saves 5 or more hours a week in the kitchen. We'll show you how meal prep can elevate your clean-eating regimen while giving you time to enjoy meals with the ones you love.

What Exactly Is "Meal Prep"?

Meal prep is the process of planning and cooking all your meals for the week to come at once. Unlike meal planning, where you simply decide what you'll eat for each meal of the week, meal prepping reserves one day to actually do all the cooking, portioning, and packing up for the entire week.

Meal prep makes clean eating convenient by turning meals into "grab-and-go" options, which is ideal for those with busy lifestyles. It allows you the freedom and flexibility to always have a clean-eating option available, even when you don't have time to cook. If you can make the simple commitment of just 2 or 3 hours of weekly meal prep at one time, we promise it will make your clean-eating lifestyle convenient, enjoyable, and sustainable.

Why Is Meal Prep Awesome?

Many of our readers say they want to eat healthier, feel better, and have more energy. A clean-eating approach to your diet can help with all three of these goals, but without a plan, it can be difficult to stick with any change long enough to see results. Committing to preparing your meals ahead will help you make healthy choices that nourish your body, honor your goals throughout your busy week, and reach your health goals.

There are many more benefits of meal prepping than those just mentioned. Convenience and improved health are the most important, but meal prep is also cost effective, time efficient, and great for portion control. Many of our readers have said that meal prep helps relieve their anxiety by eliminating uncertainty about what to eat throughout the week. Although meal prep can seem confusing at first, stick with us—the meal prep plans in part 2 will help clarify and alleviate any concerns.

Six-Step Prep

To help you reach your goals faster, we've outlined six important steps for success with clean-eating meal prep. Remember, creating a sustainable clean-eating regimen is about making choices that complement your existing lifestyle, so feel free to make adjustments as needed:

1. **Choose your prep day.** Choose any day that works for your schedule and put it in your calendar. This reaffirms your commitment to your clean-eating goals and helps ensure that other tasks don't push meal prep to the wayside.

2. **Make your plan.** We've provided the first six full weeks of complete meal prep plans for you to follow, making it easy to get started. Once you have the process down, you can develop your own weekly plans using the recipes in part 3 of this book.

3. **Go grocery shopping.** The first six weeks of meal plans include shopping lists to make your trip to the grocery store or farmers' market quick, easy,

and thorough. Whether you shop yourself or use a delivery service, it's important to procure fresh ingredients weekly before your prep day.

4. **Prepare and cook.** This step is the most labor-intensive one, but with some planning, it can be easy and a huge time-saver. In a single meal prep session, you should be able to prep 3 to 5 (or more!) recipes to enjoy all week.

5. **Portion and pack.** Every recipe in this book includes instructions on how to portion and store your prepped meals. By portioning your meals ahead, you ensure you have healthy and delicious meals ready to go, even on your busiest days.

6. **Grab and go!** For the rest of the week, your work is done! All your meals have been prepared, portioned, and packed for convenient use. Detailed instructions for assembling or reheating meals are included after every recipe.

Set Yourself Up for Success

Taking the time to set yourself up for success in the kitchen before your first meal-prep session will help make the process easier and more enjoyable. Meal prep does not require special tools or equipment—you can use the kitchen essentials you already own to prepare these recipes. If you're brand new to cooking, see the Resources section on page 166 for tips on how to stock your kitchen with basic equipment.

Kitchen Equipment

Baking sheets—From making double batches of oven-roasted protein recipes to easy sheet pan meals, we recommend at least two large rimmed baking sheets to use on prep day.

Blender—It doesn't need to be an expensive one, but having a blender will help you make smoothies, salad dressings, sauces, desserts, and more quickly and easily.

Cast-iron skillet or sauté pan—You can use either, but you'll want at least one 12-inch skillet or pan to cook stovetop recipes.

Cutting boards—We recommend having two large cutting boards, one to use with raw protein and another for produce.

Knives and utensils—Having high-quality knives (especially a chef's knife and paring knife) lets you make efficient use of your time, especially when prepping fresh meat and produce.

Measuring cups and spoons—Measuring cups and spoons serve two purposes in meal prep: to ensure accurate measuring when cooking recipes and to help guide appropriate portion sizes.

Mixing bowls—You'll need small, medium, and large bowls to use for preparing recipes.

Slow cooker, rice cooker, or electric pressure cooker (such as the Instant Pot)—Although it's not 100 percent necessary, having one of these optional tools is a worthy investment to save time prepping grains and large batches of protein.

Storage Essentials

Quality storage containers (or meal-prep containers, as we call them in this book) are an important investment for successful clean-eating meal prep. They ensure your delicious and healthy dishes stay fresh and flavorful until you are ready to eat them. Having a generous supply of meal-prep containers is important, too—you don't want to run out halfway through prepping.

If you plan to prep multiple meals for breakfast, lunch, and dinner for each weekday, you'll need at least 15 containers (3 meals a day, 5 days a week). We recommend a combination of single- and multicompartment containers, as different recipes have different storage instructions using single-, double-, or triple-compartment containers (and Mason jars). Having containers in multiple sizes is helpful, too, as you'll be packing dishes ranging from entrées to snacks to small sides of dressing.

There are countless meal-prep containers on the market today, so it's important to know what to look for. Purchase items that are microwave-, freezer-, and dishwasher-safe, as you'll be portioning, storing, and reheating in the same container.

We recommend glass meal-prep containers. Plastic containers may contain BPA, an industrial chemical that may be responsible for adverse health effects on the brain and reproductive system. For smaller storage (especially for items like dressings), we recommend small stainless-steel containers. If you use plastic storage containers, ensure they are labeled BPA-free and food-grade.

THE KEYS TO CONTINUED MEAL PREP SUCCESS

Our goal is to help you enjoy clean-eating meal prep so much that you practice it for life. To guarantee success for months and years to come, here are a few of our favorite tips and tricks.

Batch cooking: This involves doubling or tripling a recipe to store or freeze extras for later use. This cook-once, enjoy-twice method saves time and energy between preps.

Know what to freeze: When batch cooking, plan what to freeze ahead. Prepared proteins, prepared grains, fresh fruits, and most fresh vegetables freeze beautifully. Avoid freezing prepared dishes that rely on fruits and vegetables, like salads.

Learn the best ways to reheat meals: Use large glass meal-prep containers that are microwave-, dishwasher-, and freezer-safe. These containers can go straight from freezer or refrigerator to the microwave to conveniently reheat food. All recipes include reheating instructions, so your reheated meals taste just as good as the day they were made.

Reusing ingredients: In the first six weeks of meal-prep plans, you'll see that we reuse ingredients by grouping similar proteins each week. For example, in the Week 4 prep, we save time by cooking a large batch of chicken to use in three different recipes.

Storing prepped foods efficiently: Glass meal-prep containers (and glass Mason jars) are convenient because you can see exactly what's inside. This will help keep your food organized so know what you have ready to eat. Plus, they're beautiful to look at!

About the Recipes and Meal Preps

The recipes featured in this book are easy, delicious, and use simple ingredients. We enjoy them ourselves at home each week. You can accommodate many different dietary needs—gluten-free, dairy-free, nut-free, and so on—as part of clean-eating meal prep. For that reason, we made it easy to customize the recipes to fit your personal nutritional needs: Each recipe is labeled, as appropriate, with dairy-free, gluten-free, nut-free, soy-free, and vegetarian labels. If a recipe doesn't have any labels, we suggest simple modifications to meet your needs.

To make it even easier for you to settle into the clean-eating meal-prep lifestyle, we have included detailed weekly plans to help you put it all together. Chapters 3 through 5 contain six weeks of ready-for-you meal-prep plans that include a grocery shopping list, equipment list, and instructions for meal prepping and cooking day, followed by the recipes themselves. Each chapter covers two weeks of meal-prep plans, and as the chapters progress, the number of recipes per week increases. Each weekly plan is designed to help you put the moving parts together, giving you structure for developing your own routine while learning the fundamentals of meal prep.

You can use the provided meal-prep plans over and over, but at some point, you'll likely want more variety. Our hope for you is that, after the first six weeks of plans, you'll feel eager to start designing your own weekly meal-prep plans. You can interchange the recipes from the first six weeks or design your own weekly prep plan from scratch using the meal prep–friendly recipes in part 3. These recipes include staples, snacks and sweet treats, smoothies and juices, breakfast recipes, and two chapters dedicated to plant-based and animal-based protein recipes.

PART TWO

Let the Prepping Begin!

These chapters introduce you to the world of meal prep with simple-to-prepare, delicious recipes. Along with the recipes, we also provide step-by-step guidance for your meal prep day, as well as grocery shopping and equipment lists. The number of recipes per prep day increases every two weeks, slowly helping you ramp up your new routine.

The first two weeks focus on helping you prep clean-eating meals for lunch and dinner. As you get comfortable with the meal-prep process, we add breakfast and snack recipes. Everything has been designed to make this easy and, hopefully, fun. If you get stuck along the way, reach out for help at EmilyKyleNutrition.com/contact.

Happy cooking!

CHAPTER THREE

Meal Prep Plan: Weeks 1 and 2

Welcome to your very first week of meal prep. In this chapter, we cover two weeks of simple three-recipe prep featuring some of our favorite recipes. This first meal-prep chapter is the easiest to execute, with fewer recipes and lighter prep days. During this time, allow yourself to get comfortable in your kitchen. Honor the time you have set aside each week to nourish your body. Stock up on essentials. Clean out your pantry and cupboard. Maybe even turn on your favorite music and dance around while you're getting started. It's so important to build a meal-prep routine you love—that way, you'll come back to it week after week.

Week 1

	LUNCH	DINNER
DAY 1	Sweet Beet & Walnut Salad (page 22)	Ponzu Chicken & Vegetables (page 24)
DAY 2	Tuna Salad Cucumber Boats (page 23)	*Leftover* Ponzu Chicken & Vegetables
DAY 3	*Leftover* Sweet Beet & Walnut Salad	*Leftover* Tuna Salad Cucumber Boats
DAY 4	*Leftover* Tuna Salad Cucumber Boats	*Leftover* Ponzu Chicken & Vegetables
DAY 5	*Leftover* Tuna Salad Cucumber Boats	*Leftover* Ponzu Chicken & Vegetables

Week 1 Shopping List

PANTRY

- Black pepper, freshly ground
- Coconut aminos
- Garlic, granulated
- Mustard: Dijon, yellow
- Oil: avocado, extra-virgin olive, sesame
- Onion, granulated
- Red pepper flakes
- Salt
- Sugar: brown, granulated
- Vinegar: white balsamic, white wine

PRODUCE

- Apple (1)
- Beets, cooked (8 ounces)
- Broccoli florets (8 ounces)
- Celery (4 medium stalks)
- Cucumbers (4 medium)
- Dill (1 small bunch)
- Garlic (1 head)
- Lemons (3)
- Limes (2)
- Onion, white (1)
- Scallions (5)
- Snap peas (8 ounces)
- Spring mix (4 ounces)

- Chicken, boneless, skinless breast (1 pound)
- Tuna, albacore, wild-caught, in water (4 [5-ounce] cans)

DAIRY

- Cheese: goat (2 tablespoons); Parmesan, grated (1½ teaspoons)
- Yogurt, full-fat plain Greek (1 cup)

GRAINS

- Rice, brown (1 cup)

NUTS AND SEEDS

- Cashews, chopped (½ cup)
- Walnuts, chopped (¼ cup)

OTHER

- Cranberries, dried (2 tablespoons)

Equipment and Storage Vessels

- Baking sheet
- Bowls: medium, large
- Chef's knife
- Cutting board (2)
- Foil
- Fork
- Glass meal-prep containers with lids, large single-compartment (2)
- Glass meal-prep containers with lids, large two-compartment (8)

- Mason jar with lid, 1-quart wide-mouth
- Measuring cups and spoons
- Pastry brush
- Salad dressing containers, 1½-ounce stainless steel (2)
- Spoons: large, small
- Stockpot, pressure cooker, rice cooker, or electric pressure cooker
- Whisk

Step-by-Step Prep

1. Follow step 1 for the **Ponzu Chicken & Vegetables** (page 24) to start cooking the rice.

2. While the rice cooks, follow steps 1 and 2 for the **Sweet Beet & Walnut Salad** (page 22) to toast the walnuts. You'll reuse the pan for the chicken and you can keep the oven on at 400°F.

3. After the walnuts are toasted, set them aside. Move on to steps 2 through 6 of the **Ponzu Chicken & Vegetables** to get the chicken and vegetables in the oven.

4. While the **Ponzu Chicken & Vegetables** roast, prepare the **Tuna Salad Cucumber Boats** (page 23) in full.

5. Once the **Ponzu Chicken & Vegetables** are cooked, remove them from the oven and set aside to cool.

6. While the chicken and vegetables cool, make a single batch (2 cups) of **Zesty Lemon Vinaigrette** (page 83) for the **Sweet Beet & Walnut Salad**. Follow the remaining steps of the **Sweet Beet & Walnut Salad** recipe. Store the remaining dressing (1¾ cups) in an airtight container—you'll use it for prep in Week 2.

7. Once the chicken and vegetables are cooled, complete step 7 of the **Ponzu Chicken & Vegetables**.

Sweet Beet & Walnut Salad

SERVES 2
PREP TIME: 15 minutes
COOK TIME: 5 minutes

GLUTEN-FREE

SOY-FREE

VEGETARIAN

¼ cup chopped walnuts

4 tablespoons Zesty Lemon Vinaigrette (page 83)

4 ounces spring mix

8 ounces cooked beets, diced

½ cup diced apple

2 tablespoons dried cranberries

2 tablespoons goat cheese

Bursting with flavor, this hearty salad includes a variety of vibrant plant-based foods. The delicious ingredients hold up well when prepped in advance. Enjoy this salad as a plant-based entrée or pair it with a protein, such as Easy Baked Seasoned Chickpeas (page 86).

1. Preheat the oven to 400°F. Line a baking sheet with foil.

2. Spread the chopped walnuts over the prepared baking sheet and toast for 5 minutes, or until golden brown. Set aside.

3. While the walnuts toast, if needed, make the vinaigrette. Portion 2 tablespoons of vinaigrette into each of 2 (1½-ounce) stainless-steel salad dressing containers.

4. Evenly portion the spring mix into 2 large single-compartment glass meal-prep containers with tight-fitting lids. Top each serving with half of the cooked beets, diced apple, chopped walnuts, dried cranberries, and goat cheese. Cover and refrigerate.

STORAGE: Keep the undressed salad refrigerated for up to 5 days. Just before eating, pour the vinaigrette over the salad, secure the lid, and shake well to coat and combine.

INGREDIENT TIP: Cooked beets can typically be found in the produce section or salad bar of your local grocery store. If your store doesn't carry cooked beets, use no-salt-added canned whole beets instead.

PER SERVING: Calories: 423; Total Fat: 33g; Saturated Fat: 5g; Protein: 8g; Total Carbohydrates: 30g; Fiber: 6g; Sugar: 21g; Cholesterol: 7mg.

Tuna Salad Cucumber Boats

SERVES 4
PREP TIME: 15 minutes

GLUTEN-FREE
NUT-FREE
SOY-FREE

4 medium cucumbers,
  washed and dried
4 (5-ounce) cans wild
  albacore tuna in
  water, drained
4 celery stalks, finely diced
1 cup full-fat plain
  Greek yogurt
½ cup finely diced
  white onion
2 teaspoons
  yellow mustard
1 teaspoon salt
½ teaspoon freshly ground
  black pepper
½ teaspoon fresh dill, finely
  chopped (optional)

If you believe canned foods can't be a part of a clean-eating lifestyle, think again! High-quality, wild-caught canned fish such as tuna and salmon are nutritious options, offering important omega-3 fatty acids, and they're convenient to boot. This tuna salad bursts with tangy flavor and has a creamy Greek yogurt base.

1. Halve the cucumbers lengthwise and scoop out the seeds with a spoon. Discard the seeds.

2. In a medium bowl, gently flake the tuna with a fork until all large chunks are broken down.

3. Add the celery, yogurt, onion, mustard, salt, pepper, and dill (if using) and mix until all ingredients are well combined.

4. Evenly portion the tuna salad into one side of 4 large two-compartment glass meal-prep containers with tight-fitting lids. Place the cucumber halves in the adjacent compartments. (If the cucumbers are too long, halve them widthwise to fit.) Cover and refrigerate.

STORAGE: Keep refrigerated for up to 5 days. Just before eating, scoop the tuna salad into the cucumber boats to assemble.

COOKING TIP: For a smoother, creamier salad, puree the tuna in a food processor, then add the remaining ingredients. Pulse for 10-second intervals until the mixture reaches your preferred consistency.

PER SERVING: Calories: 202; Total Fat: 8g; Saturated Fat: 3g; Protein: 21g; Total Carbohydrates: 14g; Fiber: 4g; Sugar: 7g; Cholesterol: 19mg

Ponzu Chicken & Vegetables

SERVES 4
PREP TIME: 15 minutes
COOK TIME: 30 minutes

DAIRY-FREE
GLUTEN-FREE
SOY-FREE

1 cup brown rice
1 teaspoon extra-virgin
  olive oil
¼ cup coconut aminos
1½ tablespoons freshly
  squeezed lime juice
1½ teaspoons light
  brown sugar
1 teaspoon sesame oil
1 pound boneless, skinless
  chicken breast, diced into
  1-inch cubes
8 ounces broccoli florets,
  cut small
8 ounces fresh snap
  peas, trimmed
4 scallions, sliced, white and
  green parts separated
½ cup chopped cashews

Ponzu is a delicious citrus-based sauce with origins in Japanese cuisine. Store-bought ponzu sauces today are often made with soy sauce, but this pared-down take on ponzu sauce uses coconut aminos, a single-ingredient alternative to soy sauce available at most grocery stores. This delicious homemade sauce gives simple chicken and vegetables a rich, savory flavor.

1. Prepare the brown rice in a rice cooker, electric pressure cooker, or on the stovetop according to the package directions.

2. Preheat the oven to 400°F. Line a baking sheet with foil and brush it with the olive oil. Set aside.

3. In a large bowl, whisk the coconut aminos, lime juice, brown sugar, and sesame oil for 1 minute, or until the sugar dissolves.

4. Add the diced chicken to the sauce, stir well, and let marinate for at least 5 minutes while you prepare the remaining ingredients.

5. Add the broccoli, snap peas, and scallion whites to the bowl and toss well to coat thoroughly in the sauce. Transfer to the prepared baking sheet and spread into a single layer.

6. Bake for 20 minutes, or until the chicken reaches an internal temperature of 165°F. The vegetables should be tender and easily pierced with a fork.

7. Evenly portion the cooked chicken and vegetables into one side of 4 large two-compartment glass meal-prep containers with tight-fitting lids. Top each portion with scallion greens and chopped cashews. Evenly portion the cooked rice into the adjacent compartments. Cover and refrigerate.

STORAGE: Keep refrigerated for up to 5 days. Reheat individual portions in the microwave on high power for 1½ to 2 minutes just before eating.

INGREDIENT TIP: To save time, look for bags of cooked frozen brown rice or cauliflower rice in the frozen section of your grocery store. These can be microwaved in 1 to 2 minutes according to the package instructions.

PER SERVING: Calories: 452; Total Fat: 14g; Saturated Fat: 2g; Protein: 35g; Total Carbohydrates: 51g; Fiber: 5g; Sugar: 8g; Cholesterol: 80mg

Week 2

	LUNCH	DINNER
DAY 1	Spiralized Zucchini Panzanella Salad (page 29)	Steak Fajitas with Peppers & Onions (page 33)
DAY 2	Black & Blue Steak Salad (page 31)	*Leftover* Steak Fajitas with Peppers & Onions
DAY 3	*Leftover* Spiralized Zucchini Panzanella Salad	*Leftover* Black & Blue Steak Salad
DAY 4	*Leftover* Black & Blue Steak Salad	*Leftover* Steak Fajitas with Peppers & Onions
DAY 5	*Leftover* Black & Blue Steak Salad	*Leftover* Steak Fajitas with Peppers & Onions

Week 2 Shopping List

PANTRY

- Black pepper, freshly ground
- Chili powder
- Chipotle pepper, ground
- Coriander, ground
- Corn flour
- Cumin, ground
- Garlic, granulated
- Garlic powder
- Oil: olive, extra-virgin olive
- Onion, granulated
- Oregano, ground
- Paprika
- Parsley, dried
- Red pepper flakes
- Salt: kosher, table
- Turmeric, ground

PRODUCE

- Cucumbers (2 small)
- Lemon (1)
- Lettuce, romaine mix (8 ounces)
- Limes (3)
- Mushrooms, baby portabella (4 ounces)
- Onion, red (1)
- Onions, white (2)
- Peppers: bell, any color (2); jalapeño (1 small, optional)
- Radishes (4 small)
- Scallions (2)
- Tomatoes, cherry (1½ pints)
- Zucchini (2 small)

PROTEIN

- Beef, flank steak
  (2 [1-pound] steaks)

DAIRY

- Cheese: blue (½ cup); mozzarella,
  fresh (6 ounces)

GRAINS

- Bread, whole-grain (2 slices)

NUTS AND SEEDS

- Pistachios, lightly salted,
  shelled (¼ cup)

OTHER

- Roasted red bell peppers
  (1 [7-ounce] jar)

Equipment and Storage Vessels

- Airtight silicone reusable
  food bags (2)
- Baking sheet
- Bowl, large
- Chef's knife
- Cutting boards (2)
- Foil
- Glass meal-prep containers with
  lids, large single-compartment (4)
- Glass meal-prep containers with
  lids, large two-compartment (6)

- Mason jar with lid, 1-quart
  wide-mouth (1)
- Measuring cups and spoons
- Salad dressing containers,
  1½-ounce stainless steel (6)
- Skillet, cast-iron, or large sauté
  pan (12-inch)
- Spatula
- Spoon, large
- Thermometer, digital instant-read
- Tongs

Step-by-Step Prep

1. Follow steps 1 through 3 of the **Spiralized Zucchini Panzanella Salad** (page 29) to start baking the croutons.

2. While the croutons bake, prepare the **Homemade Taco Seasoning** (page 82) for the **Steak Fajitas with Peppers & Onions** (page 33). Store in a 1-quart wide-mouth Mason jar with a tight-fitting lid in the pantry—it will be used again in Weeks 3 and 4.

3. Follow step 4 for the **Spiralized Zucchini Panzanella Salad.**

4. Follow steps 1 through 3 of the **Black & Blue Steak Salad** (page 31).

5. While the steak for the **Black & Blue Steak Salad** rests, use the same cast-iron skillet and follow steps 2 through 4 of the **Steak Fajitas with Peppers & Onions** (page 33).

6. While the second steak rests for the **Steak Fajitas with Peppers & Onions,** complete steps 4 through 6 of the **Black & Blue Steak Salad.** After that, complete steps 5 through 7 for the **Spiralized Zucchini Panzanella Salad.**

7. Reuse the skillet one more time for step 5 of the **Steak Fajitas with Peppers & Onions.** Then complete steps 6 and 7.

Spiralized Zucchini Panzanella Salad

SERVES 2
PREP TIME: 15 minutes
COOK TIME: 10 minutes

NUT-FREE

SOY-FREE

VEGETARIAN

2 slices whole-grain bread, torn into 1-inch pieces

½ teaspoon extra-virgin olive oil

½ teaspoon garlic powder

¼ teaspoon dried parsley

2 small zucchini, spiralized

½ pint cherry tomatoes, quartered

½ cup diced roasted red bell pepper

4 ounces baby portabella mushrooms, sliced

2 scallions, sliced, white and green parts

4 tablespoons Zesty Lemon Vinaigrette (page 83)

6 ounces fresh mozzarella

This is our favorite salad to enjoy during summer, when fresh zucchini and tomatoes are abundant in our garden and at local farmers' markets. If you don't have a spiralizer, use a vegetable peeler to make zucchini noodles. This salad is packed with plant-based nutrition and the homemade croutons take on the flavor of the lemon vinaigrette, making for a satisfying entrée. If you're following the meal-prep plans, you will have enough vinaigrette leftover from Week 1 meal prep for this recipe.

1. Preheat the oven to 350°F. Line a baking sheet with foil.

2. Arrange the torn bread pieces in a single flat layer on the prepared baking sheet and drizzle with oil, garlic powder, and parsley. Toss gently to coat.

3. Bake the croutons for 10 minutes, stirring once halfway through, until they are toasted and golden brown. Remove from the oven and set aside to cool.

4. While the croutons bake, in a large bowl, combine the zucchini, tomatoes, roasted red bell pepper, mushrooms, and scallions. Toss well.

5. Portion 2 tablespoons of vinaigrette into each of 2 (1½-ounce) stainless-steel salad dressing containers.

CONTINUED

6. Evenly portion the undressed salad into one side of 2 large two-compartment glass meal-prep containers with tight-fitting lids. Evenly portion the fresh mozzarella into the adjacent compartments. Cover and refrigerate.

7. Once cooled, evenly portion the croutons into 2 airtight silicone reusable food bags.

STORAGE: Keep the undressed salads refrigerated for up to 5 days, each paired with a container of Zesty Lemon Vinaigrette and a bag of croutons. Just before eating, add the vinaigrette and croutons to the salad container, secure the lid, and shake well to coat and combine.

COOKING TIP: To reduce prep time, use jarred roasted red bell peppers, available at most grocery stores.

PER SERVING: Calories: 623; Total Fat: 42g; Saturated Fat: 15g; Protein: 26g; Total Carbohydrates: 34g; Fiber: 7g; Sugar: 13g; Cholesterol: 61mg

Black & Blue Steak Salad

SERVES 4
PREP TIME: 20 minutes
COOK TIME: 15 minutes

GLUTEN-FREE

SOY-FREE

1 pound flank steak

2 teaspoons freshly squeezed lemon juice

1 teaspoon salt

½ teaspoon freshly ground black pepper

2 teaspoons olive oil

8 tablespoons Zesty Lemon Vinaigrette (page 83)

1 (8-ounce) package romaine lettuce mix

2 small cucumbers, sliced

1 pint cherry tomatoes, halved

4 small radishes, thinly sliced

½ cup thinly sliced red onion

½ cup blue cheese

¼ cup lightly salted shelled pistachios

A perfect blend of plants and protein, this entrée salad features hearty blackened steak and blue cheese served over a light bed of fresh lettuce, tomato, and cucumber. Whether you enjoy it as an easy prepped lunch on the go or serve the steak hot from the skillet, this salad is sure to be a crowd-pleaser for every occasion. If you're following the meal-prep plans, you will have enough vinaigrette leftover from Week 1 meal prep for this recipe.

1. Heat a large cast-iron skillet over medium heat.

2. Coat the steak with the lemon juice and season with salt and pepper, then rub the steak with oil. Place the steak in the hot skillet. A 1-inch-thick steak will take 3 to 4 minutes per side to be cooked to medium-rare. Add 1 to 5 minutes of cook time per side to reach your desired doneness.

3. Once cooked, tightly wrap the steak in foil and set aside to rest for at least 15 minutes before slicing.

4. While the steak rests, portion 2 tablespoons of vinaigrette into each of 4 (1½-ounce) stainless-steel salad dressing containers.

5. Evenly portion the romaine lettuce mix into 4 large two-compartment glass meal-prep containers with tight-fitting lids, using the largest compartments. Top the lettuce with the cucumbers, tomatoes, radishes, red onion, blue cheese, and pistachios.

CONTINUED

6. **Very thinly slice the steak against the grain. Evenly portion the steak into the smaller side of each container. Cover and refrigerate.**

STORAGE: Keep refrigerated for up to 5 days, each paired with a container of Zesty Lemon Vinaigrette. Just before eating, top the salad with the steak and drizzle with the vinaigrette. Secure the lid and shake well to coat and combine.

COOKING TIP: We prefer this steak cold, but to enjoy it hot, microwave it on high power for up to 1 minute and serve atop the cold salad. Note that once reheated, a steak cooked to medium will be closer to medium-well.

PER SERVING: Calories: 588; Total Fat: 42g; Saturated Fat: 11g; Protein: 38g; Total Carbohydrates: 15g; Fiber: 5g; Sugar: 7g; Cholesterol: 73mg

Steak Fajitas with Peppers & Onions

SERVES 4
PREP TIME: 20 minutes
COOK TIME: 25 minutes

DAIRY-FREE
GLUTEN-FREE
NUT-FREE
SOY-FREE

2½ teaspoons Homemade
   Taco Seasoning, divided
   (page 82)
1 pound flank steak
2 tablespoons freshly
   squeezed lime
   juice, divided
2 teaspoons olive oil
2 bell peppers, any color
   cut into ½-inch strips
2 white onions, cut into
   ½-inch petals
1 small jalapeño pepper,
   thinly sliced (optional)
1 teaspoon salt

These easy steak fajitas feature lean steak and delicious caramelized peppers and onions—a zesty combination you'll look forward to for dinner night after night. Feel free to get creative with different clean eating–friendly toppings, such as tomato, lettuce, onion, and plain Greek yogurt.

1. If needed, prepare the taco seasoning.

2. Heat a large cast-iron skillet over medium heat.

3. Coat the steak with 1 tablespoon of lime juice and season with 1½ teaspoons of taco seasoning, then rub the steak with oil. Place the steak in the hot skillet. A 1-inch-thick steak will take 3 to 4 minutes per side to be cooked to medium-rare. Add 1 to 5 minutes of cook time per side to reach your desired doneness.

4. Once cooked, wrap the steak tightly in foil and set aside to rest for at least 15 minutes before slicing.

5. Return the skillet to medium heat and add the bell peppers, onions, jalapeño (if using), and salt. Cook, stirring frequently, for 8 to 15 minutes, depending on your preference for doneness. For crunchy vegetables, cook for 8 minutes; for more caramelized vegetables, cook for the full 15 minutes.

CONTINUED

6. Very thinly slice the cooked steak against the grain and return it to the skillet with the vegetables. Add the remaining 1 tablespoon of lime juice and remaining 1 teaspoon of taco seasoning. Stir until well incorporated.

7. Evenly portion the fajitas into 4 large single-compartment glass meal-prep containers with tight-fitting lids. Cover and refrigerate.

STORAGE: Keep refrigerated for up to 5 days. Reheat individual portions in the microwave on high power for 1½ to 2 minutes just before eating.

PER SERVING: Calories: 294; Total Fat: 13g; Saturated Fat: 5g; Protein: 32g; Total Carbohydrates: 11g; Fiber: 3g; Sugar: 5g; Cholesterol: 60mg

CHAPTER FOUR

Meal Prep Plan: Weeks 3 and 4

The first two weeks of meal prep helped you get comfortable in the kitchen and set you on the path to developing your new meal-prep routine. We hope you're feeling confident in your cooking skills, and more important, healthier, more energized, and less stressed throughout your busy week. In this chapter, we add an additional clean eating snack to your meal-prep regimen. This will keep you on track with your goals for the week, so you won't fall back on not-so-healthy convenience snacks. Remember, if you're not a fan of any given recipe, swap in a similar recipe from chapters 6 through 10. Choose recipes that will make you look forward to lunch and dinner every day.

WEEK 3

Mayo-Free Avocado
Deviled Eggs 39

Southwestern
Bean & Corn Salad 41

Cauliflower Rice–
Stuffed Peppers 42

Kung Pao Chicken &
Vegetables 44

WEEK 4

Caprese Salad Grain Bowl 49

Jerk-Seasoned Waldorf Salad 50

Tex-Mex Chicken Lasagna 51

Easy Chicken Cacciatore 53

Week 3

	LUNCH	DINNER	SNACK
DAY 1	Southwestern Bean & Corn Salad (page 41)	Kung Pao Chicken & Vegetables (page 44)	Mayo-Free Avocado Deviled Eggs (page 39)
DAY 2	Cauliflower Rice–Stuffed Peppers (page 42)	*Leftover* Kung Pao Chicken & Vegetables	*Leftover* Mayo-Free Avocado Deviled Eggs
DAY 3	*Leftover* Southwestern Bean & Corn Salad	*Leftover* Cauliflower Rice–Stuffed Peppers	*Leftover* Mayo-Free Avocado Deviled Eggs
DAY 4	*Leftover* Cauliflower Rice–Stuffed Peppers	*Leftover* Kung Pao Chicken & Vegetables	*Leftover* Mayo-Free Avocado Deviled Eggs
DAY 5	*Leftover* Cauliflower Rice–Stuffed Peppers	*Leftover* Kung Pao Chicken & Vegetables	*Leftover* Mayo-Free Avocado Deviled Eggs

Week 3 Shopping List

PANTRY

- Cayenne pepper
- Coconut aminos
- Garlic powder
- Oil: avocado, extra-virgin olive
- Onion, granulated
- Salt
- Sugar, light brown
- Turmeric, ground
- Vinegar: balsamic, white wine

PRODUCE

- Avocado (1 large)
- Bell peppers: any color (4), red (2)
- Carrots (2)
- Celery (1 stalk)
- Cilantro (1 small bunch)
- Ginger, fresh (1 [2-inch] piece)
- Lemon (1)
- Limes (2)
- Onion, red (1)
- Pepper, jalapeño (1 small, optional)
- Scallions (4)

PROTEIN

- Chicken, boneless, skinless breast (1 pound)

DAIRY AND EGGS

- Cheese, shredded white Cheddar (¾ cup)
- Eggs, large (8)

LEGUMES

- Black beans (2 [15-ounce] cans)
- Peanuts, dry-roasted, shelled (½ cup)

FROZEN

- Cauliflower rice, frozen (2 [1-pound] packages)
- Corn, frozen (3 cups)

OTHER

- Hemp hearts (1 tablespoon, optional)
- Sambal oelek or sriracha
- Tomatoes, crushed (1 [28-ounce] can)
- Water, filtered

Equipment and Storage Vessels

- Baking sheet
- Bowl, large
- Chef's knife
- Colander
- Cutting board (2)
- Dutch oven with lid, or other oven-safe baking dish
- Electric hand mixer
- Foil
- Fork
- Glass meal-prep containers with lids, large single-compartment (4)
- Glass meal-prep containers with lids, large two-compartment (4)
- Glass meal-prep containers with lids, small single-compartment (5)
- Mason jars with lids, half-pint (2)
- Measuring cups and spoons
- Pastry brush
- Piping bag
- Saucepan with lid, medium
- Spoons: large, small
- Thermometer, digital instant-read

Step-by-Step Prep

1. Preheat the oven to 400°F and adjust the oven racks so you can comfortably fit a sheet pan and a baking dish in the oven at the same time.

2. If not starting with cooked eggs, prepare the eggs now for **Mayo-Free Avocado Deviled Eggs** (page 39), following steps 1 through 3.

3. While the eggs cook, prepare **Southwestern Bean & Corn Salad** (page 41) in full—you should have some **Homemade Taco Seasoning** left from Week 2. Reserve the remaining bean and corn salad for the **Cauliflower Rice–Stuffed Peppers** (page 42).

4. Once the eggs are cooked, finish the recipe, following steps 4 through 6, for the **Mayo-Free Avocado Deviled Eggs** (page 39).

5. Prepare the bell peppers and follow steps 2 through 4 for the **Cauliflower Rice–Stuffed Peppers** (page 42) to get the peppers in the oven.

6. While the stuffed peppers bake, follow steps 1 through 5 of the **Kung Pao Chicken & Vegetables** (page 44). Both the stuffed peppers and the kung pao chicken will bake at the same time.

7. While the chicken and stuffed peppers bake, complete step 6 of the **Kung Pao Chicken & Vegetables** to prepare the cauliflower rice.

8. Once the **Kung Pao Chicken & Vegetables** are done, remove them from the oven and complete step 7 (depending on your timing, this may be the right time to remove the lid from the **Cauliflower Rice–Stuffed Peppers**).

9. Once the **Cauliflower Rice–Stuffed Peppers** are finished baking, complete step 5.

Mayo-Free Avocado Deviled Eggs

SERVES 5
PREP TIME: 30 minutes
COOK TIME: 25 minutes

DAIRY-FREE

GLUTEN-FREE

NUT-FREE

SOY-FREE

8 large eggs
1 large avocado, halved, pitted, and flesh scooped out
1½ tablespoons freshly squeezed lemon juice
1½ teaspoons white wine vinegar
½ teaspoon salt
¼ teaspoon garlic powder
⅛ teaspoon granulated onion
⅛ teaspoon cayenne pepper
⅛ teaspoon ground turmeric
1 tablespoon hemp hearts (optional)

Hard-boiled eggs are an ideal clean-eating meal-prep staple: They're single-ingredient, easy to prepare, and packed with protein—and they're convenient to consume on the go. These mayo-free deviled eggs bring regular hard-boiled eggs to the next level with a rich filling made with nourishing egg yolk, creamy avocado, and plenty of seasonings.

1. In a medium saucepan, combine the eggs with enough cold water to cover by 1 inch. Place the saucepan over high heat and bring the water to a full rolling boil.

2. Once boiling, turn off the heat, keep the pan on the hot burner, cover the pan, and let sit for 10 to 12 minutes.

3. Drain the water from the saucepan and run cold water over the eggs to cool them quickly and stop them from cooking further. Once cool enough to handle, peel the eggs under cold running water.

4. Halve the eggs lengthwise. Scoop the egg yolks into a medium bowl and set aside.

5. Arrange 3 egg white halves, hollow-side up, in each of 5 small single-compartment glass meal-prep containers with tight-fitting lids. (You'll have one half left over—enjoy it as a "chef snack!")

CONTINUED

6. Add the avocado, lemon juice, vinegar, salt, garlic powder, granulated onion, cayenne, and turmeric to the yolks. Mix thoroughly until no lumps remain—an electric handheld mixer works well here. Fill a piping bag with the egg yolk mixture (or use a resealable zip-top bag, cutting off one bottom corner) and evenly pipe the filling into the center of each egg white. Sprinkle with hemp hearts (if using). Cover and refrigerate.

STORAGE: Keep refrigerated for up to 5 days.

COOKING TIP: If you have them, farm-fresh eggs are great, but they are harder to peel because there is very little airspace between the membrane of the eggs and the shell. To save time on your prep day, purchase pre-cooked, peeled hard-boiled eggs, available at most grocery stores.

PER SERVING (3 HALVES): Calories: 190; Total Fat: 14g; Saturated Fat: 4g; Protein: 11g; Total Carbohydrates: 5g; Fiber: 3g; Sugar: 1g; Cholesterol: 298mg

Southwestern Bean & Corn Salad

SERVES 8

PREP TIME: 15 minutes

DAIRY-FREE

GLUTEN-FREE

NUT-FREE

SOY-FREE

VEGETARIAN

3 cups frozen sweet
  corn, thawed

2 (15-ounce) cans
  black beans, drained
  and rinsed

½ cup finely diced red onion

1 cup finely diced red
  bell pepper

1 small jalapeño pepper,
  diced (optional)

2 tablespoons freshly
  squeezed lime juice

1 tablespoon avocado oil

1 tablespoon white
  wine vinegar

2 teaspoons Homemade
  Taco Seasoning (page 82)

1 teaspoon chopped fresh
  cilantro

This lettuce-less salad is incredibly versatile and it holds up well in the refrigerator for delicious lunches all week long. Packed with plant-based protein, complex carbohydrates, and dietary fiber, this bean and corn salad is filling on its own, but it's also great served alongside another protein, such as Super-Simple Baked Chicken (page 146). If you're following the meal-prep plans, you will have enough taco seasoning left from Week 2 for this recipe.

1. In a large bowl, combine the corn, black beans, red onion, red bell pepper, jalapeño (if using), lime juice, oil, vinegar, taco seasoning, and cilantro. Mix well to fully incorporate.

2. Portion 2 (1-cup) servings of salad into each of 2 half-pint Mason jars with lids. Secure the lids tightly and refrigerate. Reserve the remaining servings for snacking and for the Cauliflower Rice–Stuffed Peppers (page 42).

STORAGE: Keep refrigerated for up to 5 days. Shake well before enjoying.

PER SERVING (1 CUP): Calories: 179; Total Fat: 3g; Saturated Fat: <1g; Protein: 8g; Total Carbohydrates: 33g; Fiber: 10g; Sugar: 3g; Cholesterol: 0mg

Cauliflower Rice–Stuffed Peppers

SERVES 4

PREP TIME: 20 minutes

COOK TIME: 1 hour

GLUTEN-FREE

NUT-FREE

SOY-FREE

VEGETARIAN

1 pound (2½ cups) frozen
cauliflower rice, thawed

2 cups Southwestern Bean
& Corn Salad (page 41)

1 (28-ounce) can crushed
tomatoes, divided

2 tablespoons Homemade
Taco Seasoning
(page 82)

¾ cup shredded white
Cheddar cheese, divided

4 bell peppers, tops cut off
and reserved (see Cook-
ing tip), seeded

Cauliflower "rice" is cauliflower chopped into pieces about the size of a grain of rice. Cauliflower is full of nutrients, making cauliflower rice a great way to add more veggies to your diet where you might otherwise consume carbohydrates. These stuffed peppers smell so good while they roast, it's tough to pack them up without taking a bite! If you're following the meal-prep plans, you will have enough taco seasoning left from Week 2 and the Southwestern Bean & Corn Salad (page 41) from this week's prep for this recipe.

1. Preheat the oven to 400°F.

2. In a large bowl, combine the cauliflower rice, bean and corn salad, 1 cup of crushed tomatoes, the taco seasoning, and ½ cup of Cheddar cheese. Stir until fully incorporated. Evenly portion the stuffing into the bell peppers, packing it in tightly.

3. Place the stuffed peppers in a Dutch oven or other oven-safe dish with a lid. Spoon the remaining crushed tomatoes over the stuffed peppers—it should spill over and create a sauce around the peppers. Top the peppers with the remaining ¼ cup of shredded cheese.

4. Cover the pot and place it in the oven for 40 minutes. Remove the lid and cook for 20 minutes more, until the stuffing reaches an internal temperature of 165°F.

5. Place 1 stuffed pepper into each of 4 large single-compartment glass meal-prep containers with tight-fitting lids. Cover and refrigerate.

STORAGE: Keep refrigerated for up to 5 days. Reheat individual portions in the microwave on high power for 1½ to 2 minutes just before eating.

COOKING TIP: Don't throw out those pepper tops. Save them to use as a base to prop up your stuffed peppers to ensure they stay upright while cooking.

PER SERVING: Calories: 301; Total Fat: 10g; Saturated Fat: 4g; Protein: 16g; Total Carbohydrates: 45g; Fiber: 14g; Sugar: 16g; Cholesterol: 21mg

Kung Pao Chicken & Vegetables

SERVES 4
PREP TIME: 15 minutes
COOK TIME: 20 minutes

DAIRY-FREE

GLUTEN-FREE

SOY-FREE

3 teaspoons extra-virgin
olive oil, divided

3 tablespoons coconut
aminos

1 tablespoon balsamic
vinegar

1 tablespoon filtered water

2 teaspoons light
brown sugar

1½ teaspoons sambal oelek
(chili paste) or sriracha

1 teaspoon minced peeled
fresh ginger

1 pound boneless, skinless
chicken breast, cut into
1-inch cubes

1 cup diced (1 inch) red
bell pepper

1 cup diced (½ inch) carrot

½ cup sliced (¼ inch) celery

4 scallions, sliced, white and
green parts separated

1 pound (2½ cups) frozen
cauliflower rice

½ cup dry-roasted
shelled peanuts

This is our take on Kung Pao chicken, a spicy, stir-fried dish well known in Chinese cooking in the United States and beyond. We use chicken, peanuts, and chili sauce and serve this dish with fresh vegetables, like broccoli and snap peas. This recipe offers a satisfying sweet-yet-spicy flavor, which pairs perfectly with the crunchy texture of peanuts and veggies.

1. Preheat the oven to 400°F. Line a baking sheet with foil and brush it with 1 teaspoon of oil. Set aside.

2. In a large bowl, combine the remaining 2 teaspoons of oil, coconut aminos, vinegar, water, brown sugar, sambal oelek, and ginger. Whisk for 1 minute, or until the brown sugar dissolves.

3. Add the chicken to the sauce, stir well, and let sit for at least 5 minutes to marinate while you prepare the remaining ingredients.

4. Add the red bell pepper, carrot, celery, and scallion whites to the bowl and toss well to coat thoroughly in the sauce. Transfer to the baking sheet, spreading into an even layer.

5. Bake for 20 minutes, or until the chicken reaches an internal temperature of 165°F. The vegetables should be tender and easily pierced with a fork.

6. While the chicken and vegetables roast, prepare the frozen cauliflower rice according to the package directions.

7. Evenly portion the chicken and vegetables into one side of 4 large two-compartment glass meal-prep containers with tight-fitting lids. Top each serving with scallion greens and peanuts. Place the cooked rice in the adjacent compartments. Cover and refrigerate.

STORAGE: Keep refrigerated for up to 5 days. Reheat individual portions in the microwave on high power for 1½ to 2 minutes just before eating.

COOKING TIP: Look for bags of cooked, frozen cauliflower rice in most grocery stores' freezer sections. Microwave for 1 to 2 minutes, according to the package directions.

PER SERVING: Calories: 345; Total Fat: 16g; Saturated Fat: 2g; Protein: 33g; Total Carbohydrates: 21g; Fiber: 7g; Sugar: 12g; Cholesterol: 80mg

Week 4

	LUNCH	DINNER	SNACK
DAY 1	Caprese Salad Grain Bowl (page 49)	Tex-Mex Chicken Lasagna (page 51)	Jerk-Seasoned Waldorf Salad (page 50)
DAY 2	Easy Chicken Cacciatore (page 53)	*Leftover* Tex-Mex Chicken Lasagna	*Leftover* Jerk-Seasoned Waldorf Salad
DAY 3	*Leftover* Caprese Salad Grain Bowl	*Leftover* Easy Chicken Cacciatore	*Leftover* Jerk-Seasoned Waldorf Salad
DAY 4	*Leftover* Easy Chicken Cacciatore	*Leftover* Tex-Mex Chicken Lasagna	*Leftover* Jerk-Seasoned Waldorf Salad
DAY 5	*Leftover* Easy Chicken Cacciatore	*Leftover* Tex-Mex Chicken Lasagna	*Leftover* Jerk-Seasoned Waldorf Salad

Week 4 Shopping List

PANTRY

- Balsamic glaze
- Basil, dried
- Black pepper, freshly ground
- Honey
- Jerk seasoning (we recommend Walkerswood)
- Oil, extra-virgin olive
- Parsley, dried
- Red pepper flakes
- Salt
- Turmeric, ground
- Vinegar, balsamic

PRODUCE

- Apples (2)
- Basil (1 large bunch)
- Bell peppers, red (2)
- Carrots (2 medium)
- Celery (3 stalks)
- Garlic (1 head)
- Grapes, red, seedless (1 bunch)
- Lemons (4)
- Onion, white (1)
- Spinach, baby (4 ounces)
- Tomatoes, cherry (1 pint)

PROTEIN

- Chicken, boneless, skinless breast (2½ pounds)

DAIRY AND EGGS

- Cheese, shredded white Cheddar (1½ cups)
- Egg, large (1)
- Mozzarella, fresh (6 ounces)
- Ricotta, whole-milk (1 cup)
- Yogurt, full-fat plain Greek (1 cup)

GRAINS

- Quinoa, dried (1 cup)

NUTS AND SEEDS

- Walnuts, shelled, toasted (½ cup)

OTHER

- Tomatoes, crushed (1 [28-ounce] can)
- Tomatoes, diced (1 [28-ounce] can)
- Tortillas, 6-inch corn (12)

Equipment and Storage Vessels

- 9-by-7-inch glass baking dish with lid
- Airtight freezer-safe container (1)
- Baking sheets (2)
- Bowls: large (1), medium (2), small (1)
- Chef's knife
- Cutting boards (2)
- Foil
- Fork
- Glass meal-prep containers with lids, large single-compartment (6)
- Glass meal-prep containers with lids, large two-compartment (4)
- Mason jars with lids, pint-size (5)
- Measuring cups and spoons
- Pastry brush
- Rice cooker
- Salad dressing containers, 1½-ounce stainless steel (2)
- Spoon, large
- Thermometer, digital instant-read
- Whisk

Step-by-Step Prep

1. Preheat the oven to 400°F.

2. In a rice cooker, prepare 1 cup dried quinoa (3 cups cooked) according to the package directions for use in the **Caprese Salad Grain Bowl** (page 49) and **Easy Chicken Cacciatore** (page 53). Set it aside to cool completely.

3. Cut all 2½ pounds of chicken into 1-inch strips. You'll use 1 pound in the **Easy Chicken Cacciatore** (page 53) and the other 1½ pounds in the **Super-Simple Baked Chicken** (page 146) for the **Jerk-Seasoned Waldorf Salad** (page 50) and the **Tex-Mex Chicken Lasagna** (page 51).

4. While the quinoa cooks, follow steps 1 through 3 to make 1½ pounds of **Super-Simple Baked Chicken** (page 146). Note that this is 1½ batches of the recipe, so you will need to adjust the ingredients: Toss the chicken with ¾ teaspoon of oil, ¾ teaspoon of salt, ¾ teaspoon of freshly squeezed lemon juice, and a scant ¼ teaspoon of pepper. Proceed as directed.

5. While the **Super-Simple Baked Chicken** bakes, complete steps 2 through 6 for the **Easy Chicken Cacciatore** (page 53) and put it in the oven (by this time, the **Super-Simple Baked Chicken** should be ready).

6. Once the **Super-Simple Baked Chicken** is cooked, remove it from the oven. Cut two-thirds (1 pound) of the chicken into 1-inch dice for the **Jerk-Seasoned Waldorf Salad** (page 50) and finely chop the rest (8 ounces) for the **Tex-Mex Chicken Lasagna.**

7. While the **Easy Chicken Cacciatore** bakes, complete steps 3 and 4 of the **Tex-Mex Chicken Lasagna** (page 51) to prep all the mixtures.

8. Once the **Easy Chicken Cacciatore** is cooked, remove it from the oven and complete step 7. Lower the oven temperature to 375°F for the **Tex-Mex Chicken Lasagna.**

9. Complete steps 5 and 6 of the **Tex-Mex Chicken Lasagna** (page 51) to get the lasagna in the oven.

10. While the lasagna cooks, follow steps 2 and 3 to complete the **Jerk-Seasoned Waldorf Salad** (page 50).

11. Once the quinoa is cooled completely, complete steps 2 through 4 of the **Caprese Salad Grain Bowl** (page 49).

12. Once the **Tex-Mex Chicken Lasagna** is cooked, complete step 7.

Caprese Salad Grain Bowl

SERVES 2
PREP TIME: 15 minutes

GLUTEN-FREE

NUT-FREE

SOY-FREE

VEGETARIAN

1 cup cooked (⅓ cup
 dried) quinoa, cooled
 completely

4 ounces baby spinach

1 cup fresh basil,
 roughly chopped

2 tablespoons extra-virgin
 olive oil

1 tablespoon freshly
 squeezed lemon juice

1 cup cherry tomatoes,
 diced

6 ounces fresh mozzarella,
 diced

1 teaspoon balsamic glaze

This hearty grain bowl pays homage to the classic flavors of caprese salad: fresh tomatoes, basil, and mozzarella. Paired with high-protein, high-fiber quinoa, this satisfying entrée-style salad is both decadent and nutritious. To make this dairy-free, dice an avocado and use it in place of the mozzarella. For more protein, pair it with an animal-based protein recipe from chapter 10.

1. If needed, cook the quinoa according to the package directions. Set aside to cool.

2. In a large bowl, toss together the spinach and basil.

3. In a small bowl, whisk the oil and lemon juice to combine. Evenly portion the dressing into 2 (1½-ounce) stainless-steel salad dressing containers.

4. Evenly divide the greens into 2 large single-compartment glass meal-prep containers with tight-fitting lids. Top with the cooked quinoa, diced tomatoes, and mozzarella. Drizzle each with ½ teaspoon of balsamic glaze. Cover and refrigerate.

STORAGE: Keep the containers of undressed salad refrigerated for up to 5 days, each paired with a container of dressing. Just before serving, pour the dressing over the salad, secure the lid, and shake well to coat and combine.

COOKING TIP: Balsamic glaze is thicker and sweeter than balsamic vinegar and it's available at most grocery stores. To make your own balsamic glaze, in a saucepan over medium heat, bring 1 cup balsamic vinegar to a boil. Reduce the heat to low and simmer until the vinegar thickens and reduces to ¼ cup.

PER SERVING: Calories: 525; Total Fat: 34g; Saturated Fat: 14g; Protein: 23g; Total Carbohydrates: 30g; Fiber: 5g; Sugar: 8g; Cholesterol: 61mg

Jerk-Seasoned Waldorf Salad

SERVES 5
PREP TIME: 20 minutes

GLUTEN-FREE

SOY-FREE

1 pound Super-Simple
   Baked Chicken
   (page 146), cut into
   1-inch dice
1 cup full-fat plain
   Greek yogurt
1 teaspoon jerk seasoning
1 teaspoon honey
1 teaspoon freshly
   squeezed lemon juice
2 cups diced (½ inch) apple
2 cups halved red
   seedless grapes
⅔ cup sliced (¼ inch) celery
½ cup toasted walnuts

This is not your average mayonnaise-drenched Waldorf salad. Our clean eating–friendly version combines protein-rich Greek yogurt with spicy Jamaican jerk seasoning, available at most grocery stores and online. Roasted chicken, grapes, apples, and toasted walnuts provide plenty of texture. To make this a full meal, serve it over a bed of rice.

1. If needed, prepare the baked chicken.

2. In a large bowl, stir together the yogurt, jerk seasoning, honey, and lemon juice to fully combine. Add the chicken, apple, grapes, celery, and walnuts and stir to coat.

3. Evenly portion the chicken salad into 5 pint-size Mason jars with tight-fitting lids. Seal the lids and refrigerate.

STORAGE: Keep refrigerated for up to 5 days.

SUBSTITUTION TIP: To make this dish vegetarian friendly, replace the chicken with 1 (14.5-ounce) can chickpeas, drained and rinsed.

PER SERVING: Calories: 296; Total Fat: 12g; Saturated Fat: 2g; Protein: 27g; Total Carbohydrates: 23g; Fiber: 3g; Sugar: 18g; Cholesterol: 71mg

Tex-Mex Chicken Lasagna

SERVES 6

PREP TIME: 20 minutes
COOK TIME: 1 hour, plus
30 minutes to rest

> GLUTEN-FREE
>
> NUT-FREE
>
> SOY-FREE

8 ounces Super-Simple
  Baked Chicken
  (page 146), finely
  chopped, divided
  (4 ounces per layer)
1 teaspoon extra-virgin
  olive oil
1 cup whole-milk ricotta,
  divided (½ cup per layer)
1 large egg
1 teaspoon salt
1 (28-ounce) can crushed
  tomatoes, divided (¾ cup
  per layer)
¼ cup Homemade Taco
  Seasoning (page 82)
12 (6-inch) corn tortillas,
  halved, divided (8 halves
  per later)
1½ cups shredded white
  Cheddar cheese, divided
  (½ cup per layer)

This easy Tex-Mex Chicken Lasagna uses corn tortillas instead of typical lasagna noodles. This hearty meal will make more than 4 servings, so freeze the additional 2 portions to have on hand for those super-busy days. If you're following the meal-prep plans, you will have enough taco seasoning left from Week 2 for this recipe.

1. If needed, prepare the baked chicken.

2. Preheat the oven to 375°F. Brush a 9-by-7-inch baking dish with oil and set aside.

3. In a medium bowl, stir together the ricotta, egg, and salt. Set aside.

4. In another medium bowl, stir together the crushed tomatoes and taco seasoning. Spread ¾ cup of tomato sauce in the prepared baking dish. Top with 8 tortilla halves, arranged in a flat layer (as you would layer lasagna noodles).

5. Layer the tortillas with ½ cup of the ricotta mixture, followed by 4 ounces of chicken, and finally ½ cup of Cheddar cheese. Repeat, layering tomato sauce, tortilla halves, ricotta, chicken, and Cheddar cheese. Top with the remaining tomato sauce, followed by any remaining Cheddar. Cover the dish with foil.

6. Bake the lasagna for 40 minutes. Remove the foil and bake, uncovered, for 20 minutes more, or until the lasagna reaches an internal temperate of 165°F. The cheese should be golden brown and bubbly. Let the lasagna rest for 30 minutes, then cut it into 6 slices.

CONTINUED

7. Place 1 slice into each of 4 large single-compartment glass meal-prep containers with tight-fitting lids. Cover and refrigerate. Freeze the remaining two portions in an airtight freezer-safe container for up to 3 months.

STORAGE: Keep refrigerated for up to 5 days. Reheat individual portions in the microwave on high power for 1½ to 2 minutes just before eating. Thaw frozen portions in the refrigerator overnight before reheating, or reheat from frozen in the microwave on high power for 4 to 5 minutes.

REUSE TIP: This recipe is great for using up leftover vegetables you have in the refrigerator. Leftover cooked greens, peppers, mushrooms, beans, and corn all make excellent additions.

PER SERVING: Calories: 402; Total Fat: 19g; Saturated Fat: 9g; Protein: 25g; Total Carbohydrates: 38g; Fiber: 6g; Sugar: 8g; Cholesterol: 106mg

Easy Chicken Cacciatore

SERVES 4
PREP TIME: 15 minutes
COOK TIME: 30 minutes

DAIRY-FREE

GLUTEN-FREE

NUT-FREE

SOY-FREE

2 cups cooked (⅔ cup dried) quinoa

1 teaspoon extra-virgin olive oil

1 (28-ounce) can diced tomatoes with juices

1 tablespoon minced garlic

1 tablespoon balsamic vinegar

1 teaspoon salt

1 teaspoon freshly ground black pepper

1 teaspoon dried basil

1 teaspoon dried parsley

1 teaspoon ground turmeric

⅛ teaspoon red pepper flakes

1 pound boneless, skinless chicken breast, cut into 1-inch-thick strips

2 red bell peppers, cut into ½-inch strips

2 medium carrots, sliced into ⅛-inch pieces on the bias

½ large white onion, cut into ½-inch strips

This chicken cacciatore is our version of the classic Italian dish made with chicken (or other meat) braised in a hearty tomato sauce. Simple to put together yet sophisticated in flavor, this easy one-pan meal will become a meal-prep favorite.

1. If needed, cook the quinoa according to the package directions. Set aside.

2. Preheat the oven to 400°F. Line a baking sheet with foil and brush it with oil. Set aside.

3. In a large bowl, stir together the tomatoes and their juices, garlic, vinegar, salt, pepper, basil, parsley, turmeric, and red pepper flakes.

4. Add the chicken to the tomato sauce mixture and stir to incorporate. Marinate at least 5 minutes while you prepare the remaining ingredients.

5. Add the red bell peppers, carrots, and onion to the bowl and toss to coat thoroughly in the tomato sauce. Transfer the mixture to the prepared baking sheet and spread it into an even layer.

6. Roast for 30 minutes, or until the chicken reaches an internal temperature of 165°F. The vegetables should be tender and easily pierced with a fork.

7. Evenly divide the chicken into the larger side of 4 large two-compartment glass meal-prep containers with tight-fitting lids. Place the cooked quinoa in the adjacent compartment. Cover and refrigerate.

STORAGE: Keep refrigerated for up to 5 days. Reheat individual portions in the microwave on high power for 1½ to 2 minutes just before eating.

PER SERVING: Calories: 337; Total Fat: 5g; Saturated Fat: 1g; Protein: 32g; Total Carbohydrates: 40g; Fiber: 9g; Sugar: 11g; Cholesterol: 80mg

CHAPTER FIVE

Meal Prep Plan: Weeks 5 and 6

Welcome to chapter 5—at this point, you're well-versed in meal prep and ready to bump it up another notch. In this chapter, for Weeks 5 and 6, you'll prepare five recipes each meal-prep day, so you can be fully stocked for breakfast, lunch, dinner, and snacks. Although these two weeks have the most involved prep, have no fear—the featured recipes are quick and simple and designed to help you make the most of your time spent in the kitchen without feeling like you have to spend all day there. Once you decide how many recipes you're comfortable prepping per week, you can start designing your own meal-prep plans with the DIY Prep Planning guide on page 76 using the recipes in part 3 of the book.

Week 5

	BREAKFAST	LUNCH	DINNER	SNACK
DAY 1	Honey-Berry Yogurt Parfait (page 59)	Avocado BLT Salad (page 61)	Chicken & Broccoli Dijon Rice (page 64)	Energy-Boosting Trail Mix (page 60)
DAY 2	*Leftover* Honey-Berry Yogurt Parfait	Garlic Tofu & Brussels Sprouts (page 62)	*Leftover* Chicken & Broccoli Dijon Rice	*Leftover* Energy-Boosting Trail Mix
DAY 3	*Leftover* Honey-Berry Yogurt Parfait	*Leftover* Avocado BLT Salad	*Leftover* Garlic Tofu & Brussels Sprouts	*Leftover* Energy-Boosting Trail Mix
DAY 4	*Leftover* Honey-Berry Yogurt Parfait	*Leftover* Garlic Tofu & Brussels Sprouts	*Leftover* Chicken & Broccoli Dijon Rice	*Leftover* Energy-Boosting Trail Mix
DAY 5	*Leftover* Honey-Berry Yogurt Parfait	*Leftover* Garlic Tofu & Brussels Sprouts	*Leftover* Chicken & Broccoli Dijon Rice	*Leftover* Energy-Boosting Trail Mix

Week 5 Shopping List

PANTRY

- Balsamic glaze
- Black pepper, freshly ground
- Chives, dried
- Cooking spray, nonstick
- Dill, dried
- Garlic powder
- Honey
- Italian seasoning
- Oil, extra-virgin olive
- Onion powder
- Parsley, dried
- Pumpkin pie spice
- Red pepper flakes (optional)
- Salt
- Turmeric, ground
- Vinegar: balsamic, white

PRODUCE

- Avocado (1)
- Blackberries (1½ cups)
- Broccoli florets (12 ounces)
- Brussels sprouts (1 pound)
- Garlic (1 head)
- Lemons (2)
- Lettuce, Boston Bibb or butter (1 small head, or 4 ounces)
- Scallions (2)
- Strawberries (1¼ cups)
- Tomatoes, cherry (½ pint)

PROTEIN

- Bacon, uncured (6 slices)
- Chicken, boneless, skinless breast (1 pound)

DAIRY

- Milk, full-fat (1 tablespoon)
- Yogurt: full-fat plain Greek (1 cup), nonfat plain Greek (2½ cups)

GRAINS

- Rice, brown (1 cup)

LEGUMES

- Tofu, extra-firm, organic (1 [14-ounce] package)

NUTS AND SEEDS

- Chia seeds (2 tablespoons)
- Coconut flakes, unsweetened (½ cup)
- Hemp seeds (½ cup)
- Pumpkin seeds, roasted, salted (¼ cup)
- Walnuts, chopped (½ cup)

OTHER

- Cherries, dried (1 cup)
- Chicken broth (3 cups)
- Chocolate chips, dark (½ cup)
- Mustard, Dijon (2 tablespoons)

Equipment and Storage Vessels

- Airtight silicone reusable food bags (5)
- Baking sheet
- Bowls: small, large
- Chef's knife
- Cutting boards (2)
- Dutch oven with lid, or other large pot with lid
- Foil
- Glass meal-prep containers with lids, large single-compartment (10)
- Kitchen towels (2)
- Mason jars with lids: 1-quart wide-mouth (2), half-pint with lids (5)
- Measuring cups and spoons
- Paper towels
- Salad dressing containers, 1½-ounce stainless steel (2)
- Saucepan, medium
- Skillet, medium
- Spoon, large
- Thermometer, digital instant-read
- Tongs
- Whisk

Step-by-Step Prep

1. Follow steps 1 and 2 for the **Chia Seed Fruit Preserves** (page 87) used in the **Honey-Berry Yogurt Parfait** (step 1 of the main recipe). Set aside to cool for 30 minutes.

2. While the **Chia Seed Fruit Preserves** cool, follow all steps to complete the **Energy-Boosting Trail Mix** (page 60).

3. Follow step 1 for the **Avocado BLT Salad** (page 61) to cook the bacon.

4. While the bacon cools, follow all steps for the **Creamy Ranch Dressing** (page 84) used in the **Avocado BLT Salad**. Portion 2 servings of dressing into containers for the **Avocado BLT Salad** (step 2 in the recipe). Refrigerate the remaining dressing (¾ cup) in an airtight container—you'll use it again during Week 6.

5. Complete steps 3 and 4 to finish packing the **Avocado BLT Salad**.

6. Preheat the oven to 400°F and follow step 1 for the **Garlic Tofu & Brussels Sprouts** (page 62). While the oven preheats, follow steps 2 and 3 to complete the **Honey-Berry Yogurt Parfait** (page 59). You'll have about ¼ cup of **Chia Seed Fruit Preserves** left over for another use.

CONTINUED

7. Follow steps 2 through 4 for the **Garlic Tofu & Brussels Sprouts** (page 62).

8. While the **Garlic Tofu & Brussels Sprouts** roasts, follow steps 1 through 5 for the **Chicken & Broccoli Dijon Rice** (page 64).

9. While the **Chicken & Broccoli Dijon Rice** is simmering, follow steps 5 and 6 to complete the **Garlic Tofu & Brussels Sprouts**.

10. Follow step 6 to complete the **Chicken & Broccoli Dijon Rice**.

Honey-Berry Yogurt Parfait

SERVES 5
PREP TIME: 15 minutes

GLUTEN-FREE

NUT-FREE

SOY-FREE

VEGETARIAN

Heaping ¾ cup Chia Seed
  Fruit Preserves (page 87)
2½ cups nonfat plain
  Greek yogurt
1¼ cups sliced fresh
  strawberries
5 teaspoons honey

This parfait contains the optimal combination of protein, fat, and carbohydrates to help keep you full and energized all morning. The beauty of this quick and easy-to-prep option is you can customize it week after week, trying different flavor combinations using whatever fruit is in season. Beyond strawberries, we love to top this parfait with fresh or frozen blueberries, peaches, and cherries.

1. If needed, prepare the preserves.

2. Portion ½-cup servings of yogurt into each of 5 half-pint Mason jars with lids.

3. Top each yogurt serving with 2 generous tablespoons of preserves, followed by ¼ cup of sliced strawberries, and, finally, 1 teaspoon of honey. Secure the lids and refrigerate.

STORAGE: Keep refrigerated for up to 5 days. Stir the ingredients before enjoying.

INGREDIENT TIP: If appropriate for your dietary needs, opt for a fat-free, 2%, or even dairy-free yogurt alternative.

PER SERVING: Calories: 158; Total Fat: 2g; Saturated Fat: <1g; Protein: 14g; Total Carbohydrates: 23g; Fiber: 4g; Sugar: 19g; Cholesterol: 6mg

Energy-Boosting Trail Mix

SERVES 5

PREP TIME: 10 minutes

GLUTEN-FREE

SOY-FREE

VEGETARIAN

½ cup chopped walnuts

½ cup dark chocolate chips

½ cup dried cherries

½ cup hemp seeds

½ cup unsweetened
   coconut flakes

Homemade trail mix is a meal-prep staple—it's lightweight, easy to pack and store, and convenient to eat on the go. Dense in nutrients as well as calories from a combination of fats, carbs, and protein, trail mix is a perfect energizing pre- or post-workout snack.

In a large bowl, stir together the walnuts, chocolate chips, dried cherries, hemp seeds, and coconut flakes. Portion the trail mix into 5 airtight silicone reusable food bags.

STORAGE: Store in the pantry for up to 1 month.

SUBSTITUTION TIP: Make this recipe your own by adding your favorite clean-eating ingredients, like different nuts, seeds, or dried fruit.

PER SERVING: Calories: 371; Total Fat: 26g; Saturated Fat: 9g; Protein: 9g; Total Carbohydrates: 29g; Fiber: 5g; Sugar: 21g; Cholesterol: 2mg

Avocado BLT Salad

SERVES 2
PREP TIME: 20 minutes
COOK TIME: 10 minutes

GLUTEN-FREE
NUT-FREE
SOY-FREE

6 uncured bacon slices
4 tablespoons Creamy
 Ranch Dressing (page 84)
1 avocado, peeled, halved,
 pitted, and diced
1 teaspoon freshly
 squeezed lemon juice
4 ounces (about 1 small
 head) butter lettuce,
 chopped
½ pint cherry tomatoes,
 halved
¼ cup thinly sliced scallion,
 white and green parts

Perfect for a busy work week, this salad is so fresh and delicious you'll find yourself craving it at all hours of the day. This meal bursts with fresh tomatoes, creamy avocado, and crunchy Bibb lettuce and is topped with a small amount of crispy bacon. It makes a satisfying entrée meal.

1. In a medium skillet over medium-high heat, cook the bacon for about 10 minutes, turning, or until it is cooked through. Transfer to a paper towel to absorb the grease and cool. Once the bacon is cool enough to handle, crumble it into bite-size pieces.

2. While the bacon cools, if needed, make the dressing. Portion 2 tablespoons of dressing into each of 2 (1½-ounce) stainless-steel salad dressing containers.

3. In a small bowl, toss the diced avocado in lemon juice. This will keep it from browning once stored.

4. Evenly portion the butter lettuce into 2 large single-compartment glass meal-prep containers with tight-fitting lids. Top each serving of lettuce with avocado, tomatoes, scallions, and crumbled bacon. Cover and refrigerate.

STORAGE: Keep the undressed salads refrigerated for up to 5 days, each paired with a container of Creamy Ranch Dressing. When ready to eat, pour the dressing over the salad, secure the lid, and shake well to coat and combine.

REUSE TIP: Save the leftover bacon grease to reuse as a bacon-flavored cooking oil in other recipes.

PER SERVING: Calories: 283; Total Fat: 21g; Saturated Fat: 5g; Protein: 14g; Total Carbohydrates: 14g; Fiber: 7g; Sugar: 5g; Cholesterol: 29mg

Garlic Tofu & Brussels Sprouts

SERVES 4
PREP TIME: 20 minutes
COOK TIME: 30 minutes

DAIRY-FREE
GLUTEN-FREE
NUT-FREE
VEGETARIAN

Nonstick cooking spray
1 (14-ounce) package
   extra-firm organic tofu,
   drained and cut into
   1-inch pieces
2 tablespoons balsamic
   vinegar
1 tablespoon extra-virgin
   olive oil plus 1 teaspoon
1 tablespoon minced garlic
¼ teaspoon salt
¼ teaspoon freshly ground
   black pepper
1 pound Brussels sprouts,
   quartered
½ cup dried cherries
¼ cup roasted salted
   pumpkin seeds
1 tablespoon balsamic
   glaze

Tofu is a delicious high-protein source to add more plant-based nutrition into your diet. Paired with crunchy Brussels sprouts, sweet cranberries, and salty pumpkin seeds, this easy sheet-pan meal is bursting with flavor and texture. If you're not a fan of tofu, swap it for 1 pound of cooked chicken breast, diced into 1-inch pieces.

1. Preheat the oven to 400°F. Line a large baking sheet with foil and coat it with cooking spray. Set aside.

2. Place the tofu pieces between 2 clean towels and press them gently. Let rest for 15 minutes to wick away additional moisture.

3. In a large bowl, whisk the vinegar, 1 tablespoon of oil, the garlic, salt, and pepper to incorporate. Add the tofu and Brussels sprouts and toss gently to coat thoroughly. Transfer the ingredients to the prepared baking sheet and spread into an even layer.

4. Roast for 20 minutes.

5. Remove the sheet pan from the oven and toss its contents. Sprinkle the cherries and pumpkin seeds in an even layer on top of the Brussels sprouts and tofu. Return to the oven and roast for 10 minutes more. Remove from the oven and drizzle with balsamic glaze. Toss to coat thoroughly.

6. Evenly portion the tofu and vegetables into 4 large single-compartment glass meal-prep containers with tight-fitting lids. Cover and refrigerate.

STORAGE: Keep refrigerated for up to 5 days. Reheat individual portions in the microwave on high power for 1½ to 2 minutes just before eating.

INGREDIENT TIP: Many commercially available soybeans are genetically modified, including some used in tofu. When you buy tofu that is certified organic, the label also verifies no GMO crops were used.

PER SERVING: Calories: 317; Total Fat: 13g; Saturated Fat: 2g; Protein: 17g; Total Carbohydrates: 35g; Fiber: 7g; Sugar: 20g; Cholesterol: 0mg

Chicken & Broccoli Dijon Rice

SERVES 4
PREP TIME: 15 minutes
COOK TIME: 25 minutes

1 tablespoon extra-virgin
  olive oil
1 cup brown rice
3 cups chicken broth
2 tablespoons
  Dijon mustard
½ teaspoon salt
½ teaspoon ground
  turmeric
½ teaspoon Italian
  seasoning
¼ teaspoon freshly ground
  black pepper
¼ teaspoon red pepper
  flakes (optional)
12 ounces broccoli florets,
  cut into bite-size pieces
2 teaspoons minced garlic
1 pound boneless, skinless
  chicken breast, cut into
  1-inch pieces

This hearty chicken-and-rice dish is the epitome of clean eating comfort food. Cooked in a creamy Dijon mustard sauce, this recipe hits the spot on winter days or chilly nights. The best part about this recipe is that it's a one-pan dish, so it's perfect for busy prep days and easy to clean up.

1. In a Dutch oven or other large pot or pan with a lid over medium heat, warm the oil.

2. Add the rice and toast for about 2 minutes, until golden brown, stirring frequently.

3. Pour in the chicken broth and stir in the Dijon, salt, turmeric, Italian seasoning, black pepper, and red pepper flakes (if using). Turn the heat to medium-high and bring the mixture to a boil.

4. Stir in the broccoli florets and garlic. Return the heat to low, cover the pot, and simmer for 5 minutes.

5. Add the chicken, stir well, re-cover the pot, and simmer for 15 more minutes, or until the chicken reaches an internal temperature of 165°F and the rice is tender.

6. Evenly portion the chicken, broccoli, and rice into 4 large single-compartment glass meal-prep containers with tight-fitting lids. Cover and refrigerate.

STORAGE: Keep refrigerated for up to 5 days. Reheat individual portions in the microwave on high power for 1½ to 2 minutes just before eating.

COOKING TIP: Use a very large pan—we recommend a Dutch oven—to cook this one-pot recipe, as the rice expands in volume as it cook.

PER SERVING: Calories: 358; Total Fat: 9g; Saturated Fat: 1g; Protein: 32g; Total Carbohydrates: 41g; Fiber: 5g; Sugar: 2g; Cholesterol: 84mg

Week 6

	BREAKFAST	LUNCH	DINNER	SNACK
DAY 1	Green Tea & Ginger Overnight Oats (page 69)	Crunchy Kale Salad (page 71)	Italian Sausage Sheet Pan Dinner (page 74)	Mediterranean Snack Box (page 70)
DAY 2	*Leftover* Green Tea & Ginger Overnight Oats	Chicken Pesto Pasta (page 72)	*Leftover* Italian Sausage Sheet Pan Dinner	*Leftover* Mediterranean Snack Box
DAY 3	*Leftover* Green Tea & Ginger Overnight Oats	*Leftover* Crunchy Kale Salad	*Leftover* Chicken Pesto Pasta	*Leftover* Mediterranean Snack Box
DAY 4	*Leftover* Green Tea & Ginger Overnight Oats	*Leftover* Chicken Pesto Pasta	*Leftover* Italian Sausage Sheet Pan Dinner	*Leftover* Mediterranean Snack Box
DAY 5	*Leftover* Green Tea & Ginger Overnight Oats	*Leftover* Chicken Pesto Pasta	*Leftover* Italian Sausage Sheet Pan Dinner	*Leftover* Mediterranean Snack Box

Week 6 Shopping List

PANTRY

- Black pepper, freshly ground
- Honey
- Maple syrup
- Oil, extra-virgin olive
- Salt

PRODUCE

- Brussels sprouts, shredded (1 cup)
- Cabbage, red or green, shredded (1 cup)
- Carrots, baby (2 pounds)
- Carrots, matchstick cut (½ cup)
- Cucumbers, mini, seedless (5)
- Garlic, minced (1 head)
- Ginger, fresh (1 [2-inch] piece)
- Kale, chopped (2 cups)
- Lemons (2)
- Olives, green or Kalamata (10 ounces)
- Onion, white (1)
- Peppers: bell, any color (2); mini (1 pound)
- Radicchio (1 head)
- Sweet potatoes (1½ pounds)

PROTEIN

- Chicken, boneless, skinless breast (1 pound)
- Italian sausage, links (1 pound)

DAIRY

- Cheese, Pecorino Romano, fresh grated (1 cup)
- Mozzarella, fresh, small balls (*ciliegini*; 10 ounces)

GRAINS

- Oats, quick-cooking (2½ cups)
- Pasta, penne, whole-wheat (8 ounces)

NUTS AND SEEDS

- Chia seeds (5 teaspoons)
- Pistachios, salted, shelled (5 ounces)
- Pumpkin seeds, salted, roasted (¼ cup)

OTHER

- Pesto (½ cup)
- Raisins, golden (¼ cup)
- Tea bags, green (5)

Equipment and Storage Vessels

- Baking sheet
- Bowls: small, medium, large
- Chef's knife
- Colander
- Cutting boards (2)
- Foil
- Glass meal-prep containers with lids, large single-compartment (10)
- Glass meal-prep containers with lids, large three-compartment (5)
- Mason jars with lids, pint-size (5)
- Measuring cups and spoons
- Pastry brush
- Salad dressing containers, 1½-ounce stainless steel (2)
- Saucepans: medium, large
- Spoon, large
- Thermometer, digital instant-read

Step-by-Step Prep

1. Follow step 1 for the **Chicken Pesto Pasta** (page 72), preheating the oven to 400°F and preparing a baking sheet. You'll reuse the baking sheet for the **Italian Sausage Sheet Pan Dinner.**

2. While the oven preheats, follow all steps to assemble the **Mediterranean Snack Box** (page 70).

3. Follow steps 2 and 3 for the **Chicken Pesto Pasta** to get the chicken in the oven. While the chicken bakes, follow step 4 to cook the pasta.

4. While the pasta cooks, follow all steps for the **Green Tea & Ginger Overnight Oats** (page 69).

5. The chicken and pasta should be ready around the same time. Once they are, follow steps 5 through 7 to complete the **Chicken Pesto Pasta** (you can keep the oven at 400°F).

6. Re-line the same baking sheet with foil and brush it with olive oil for the **Italian Sausage Sheet Pan Dinner** (page 74). Complete steps 2 through 7, roasting the sweet potatoes, then adding the seasoned sausage.

7. While the sausage roasts, follow all steps for the **Crunchy Kale Salad** (page 71). You should have leftover **Creamy Ranch Dressing** from Week 5.

8. Once the sausage is cooked, follow step 8 to complete the **Italian Sausage Sheet Pan Dinner.**

Green Tea & Ginger Overnight Oats

SERVES 5
PREP TIME: 15 minutes, plus 4 hours to soak

DAIRY-FREE

GLUTEN-FREE

NUT-FREE

SOY-FREE

VEGETARIAN

2½ cups quick-cooking oats
5 teaspoons chia seeds
5 teaspoons honey
1¼ teaspoons minced peeled fresh ginger
5 green tea bags
5 cups boiling water

Overnight oats are a clean-eating meal prepper's dream—all the cooking is done for you while you sleep! This tasty green tea and ginger version boasts plenty of antioxidants and the spiced-and-sweet combination of ginger and honey flavor a delicious breakfast you'll be excited to wake up to.

1. In each of 5 pint-size Mason jars with tight-fitting lids, place ½ cup of oats, 1 teaspoon of chia seeds, 1 teaspoon of honey, ¼ teaspoon of ginger, and 1 green tea bag.

2. Pour 1 cup of boiling water over the oats in each jar. Secure the lids and shake well to combine.

3. Refrigerate the jars for at least 4 hours, ideally overnight, before serving.

STORAGE: Keep refrigerated for up to 5 days. These oats can be warmed before enjoying or served cold. To reheat, microwave on high power for 1 to 1½ minutes. The mixture will continue to thicken the longer it sits, so add hot water, 1 tablespoon of at a time, to thin the oats, as needed.

SUBSTITUTION TIP: Instead of green tea and ginger, pair these oats with any delicious flavors you can think of, such as any fresh fruit or nut butter. We love to stir in 1 tablespoon of Chia Seed Fruit Preserves (page 87).

PER SERVING: Calories: 196; Total Fat: 4g; Saturated Fat: 1g; Protein: 6g; Total Carbohydrates: 35g; Fiber: 6g; Sugar: 6g; Cholesterol: 0mg

Mediterranean Snack Box

SERVES 5

PREP TIME: 15 minutes

GLUTEN-FREE

SOY-FREE

VEGETARIAN

10 ounces fresh mozzarella balls (*ciliegini*)

10 ounces green or Kalamata olives

1 teaspoon extra-virgin olive oil

25 baby carrots

15 mini bell peppers

5 mini cucumbers, sliced

5 ounces salted shelled pistachios

This snack is our favorite clean-eating option to grab when an afternoon snack craving hits. Salty olives and pistachios paired with fresh mozzarella and crunchy vegetables make the perfect satisfying savory snack. Feel free to serve with other fresh vegetables here to use up what you already have on hand.

1. In a medium bowl, gently stir together the mozzarella, olives, and oil. Evenly portion the cheese and olive mixture into the medium compartments of 5 large three-compartment glass meal-prep containers with tight-fitting lids.

2. Place 5 baby carrots, 3 mini bell peppers, and 1 sliced mini cucumber into the largest compartment of the meal-prep containers.

3. Place 1 ounce of pistachios in the smallest compartment of each container. Cover and refrigerate.

STORAGE: Keep refrigerated for up to 5 days.

SUBSTITUTION TIP: If you're making substitutions for the olive and cheese mixture, be sure to choose a protein-rich alternative to help keep you full. Our favorite swaps are Chipotle Taco Hummus (page 85) and Easy Baked Seasoned Chickpeas (page 86).

PER SERVING: Calories: 444; Total Fat: 33g; Saturated Fat: 9g; Protein: 19g; Total Carbohydrates: 21g; Fiber: 8g; Sugar: 9g; Cholesterol: 40mg

Crunchy Kale Salad

SERVES 2
PREP TIME: 15 minutes

GLUTEN-FREE
NUT-FREE
SOY-FREE
VEGETARIAN

4 tablespoons Creamy
  Ranch Dressing
  (page 84)
2 cups chopped kale
1 cup chopped radicchio
1 cup shredded Brussels
  sprouts
½ cup matchstick carrots
1 cup shredded red or
  green cabbage
¼ cup golden raisins
¼ cup roasted salted
  pumpkin seeds

Salads should never be boring and this crunchy kale version is packed with plant-based nutrients (like dietary fiber) and a ton of flavor. We love to make this salad when we have fresh kale available in our garden, but use any combination of lettuces you have left over from other recipes. For extra protein, add leftover chicken or Easy Baked Seasoned Chickpeas (page 86). If you're following the meal-prep plans, you will have enough Creamy Ranch Dressing (page 84) leftover from Week 5 for this recipe.

1. If needed, make the dressing. Portion 2 tablespoons of ranch dressing into each of 2 (1½-ounce) stainless-steel salad dressing containers.

2. In a large bowl, toss together the kale, radicchio, Brussels sprouts, carrots, and cabbage. Evenly portion the salad mixture into 2 large single-compartment glass meal-prep containers with tight-fitting lids.

3. Top each serving with raisins and pumpkin seeds. Cover and refrigerate.

STORAGE: Keep the undressed salads refrigerated for up to 5 days, each paired with a container of Creamy Ranch Dressing. Just before eating, pour the dressing over the salad, secure the lid, and shake well to coat and combine.

SUBSTITUTION TIP: For an equally delicious dairy-free variation, skip the Creamy Ranch Dressing and serve this salad with Zesty Lemon Vinaigrette (page 83).

PER SERVING: Calories: 241; Total Fat: 10g; Saturated Fat: 3g; Protein: 11g; Total Carbohydrates: 28g; Fiber: 6g; Sugar: 19g; Cholesterol: 5mg

Chicken Pesto Pasta

SERVES 4
PREP TIME: 10 minutes
COOK TIME: 25 minutes

GLUTEN-FREE

SOY-FREE

1 teaspoon extra-virgin
olive oil

1 pound boneless, skinless
chicken breast, cut into
1-inch pieces

8 tablespoons
pesto, divided

8 ounces dried
whole-wheat
penne pasta

1 cup freshly grated
Pecorino Romano
cheese, divided

1 teaspoon freshly cracked
black pepper

This delicious, easy-to-make pasta dish is perfect for those days when you're craving comfort food. Prepared with lean chicken and vibrant pesto, a serving of this pasta fits into the clean-eating lifestyle when paired with a side salad and enjoyed in moderation.

1. Preheat the oven to 400°F. Line a large baking sheet with foil and brush it with oil. Set aside.

2. In a large bowl, combine the chicken with 3 tablespoons of pesto. Toss to coat thoroughly. Spread the chicken in an even layer on the prepared baking sheet.

3. Roast for 15 to 20 minutes, or until the chicken reaches an internal temperature of 165°F. Set aside.

4. While the chicken roasts, cook the pasta according to the package directions for al dente. Reserve 2 cups of pasta cooking water, drain the pasta, and set the pasta and reserved water aside.

5. In a large heatproof bowl, combine ¾ cup of Pecorino Romano cheese, the remaining 5 tablespoons of pesto, and the pepper. Stir in the warm pasta and mix well until all ingredients are incorporated. Add the hot chicken and stir to incorporate.

6. One tablespoon at a time, stir in the reserved pasta water. Continue adding water in small amounts and stirring until the cheese is melted and you have a smooth, creamy pasta sauce (you won't use all the pasta water).

7. Evenly portion the pasta into 4 large single-compartment glass meal-prep containers with tight-fitting lids. Garnish with the remaining ¼ cup of cheese. Cover and refrigerate.

STORAGE: Keep refrigerated for up to 5 days. Reheat individual portions in the microwave on high power for 1½ to 2 minutes just before eating.

INGREDIENT TIP: When shopping for prepared pesto at the grocery store, check the ingredient label to be sure there are no artificial preservatives or additives—versions in the refrigerated section are more likely to be made with clean eating–friendly ingredients.

PER SERVING: Calories: 577; Total Fat: 28g; Saturated Fat: 9g; Protein: 42g; Total Carbohydrates: 44g; Fiber: 6g; Sugar: 2g; Cholesterol: 114mg

Italian Sausage Sheet Pan Dinner

SERVES 4
PREP TIME: 15 minutes
COOK TIME: 40 minutes

DAIRY-FREE
GLUTEN-FREE
NUT-FREE
SOY-FREE

3 teaspoons extra-virgin
  olive oil, divided
1½ pounds sweet potatoes,
  peeled and cut into
  ½-inch dice
1 teaspoon salt, divided
1 teaspoon freshly ground
  black pepper, divided
3 tablespoons maple syrup
2 tablespoons freshly
  squeezed lemon juice
1 teaspoon minced garlic
1 pound Italian sausage
  links, cut into
  2-inch pieces
2 bell peppers, any color,
  cut into ½-inch strips
1 white onion, cut into
  ½-inch petals

This simple-but-sophisticated Italian sausage dinner features vibrant bell peppers and onions, roasted sweet and savory sweet potatoes, and delicious Italian sausage. The ultimate clean-eating meal-prep feast, this sheet-pan dinner is just as easy to clean up as it is to make—it will quickly become one of your new favorites.

1. Preheat the oven to 400°F. Line a large baking sheet with foil and brush it with 1 teaspoon of oil. Set aside.

2. In a large bowl, combine the sweet potatoes, 1 teaspoon of oil, ½ teaspoon of salt, and ½ teaspoon of pepper and toss to coat. Spread the sweet potatoes on the prepared baking sheet in an even layer. Reserve the bowl.

3. Roast the sweet potatoes for 10 minutes.

4. While the sweet potatoes roast, in the same large bowl, combine the remaining 1 teaspoon of oil, remaining ½ teaspoon of salt, remaining ½ teaspoon of pepper, maple syrup, lemon juice, and garlic. Whisk to fully incorporate.

5. Add the sausage, bell peppers, and onion to the bowl and toss until coated thoroughly.

6. After 10 minutes, remove the sweet potatoes from the oven. Add the sausage mixture to the sheet pan, toss to combine it with the sweet potatoes, and spread into an even layer.

7. Return the sheet pan to the oven and roast for 30 more minutes, or until the peppers and onion are tender and the sausage reaches an internal temperature of 165°F.

8. Evenly portion the meal into 4 large single-compartment glass meal-prep containers with tight-fitting lids. Cover and refrigerate.

STORAGE: Keep refrigerated for up to 5 days. Reheat individual portions in the microwave on high power for 1½ to 2 minutes just before eating.

INGREDIENT TIP: Adjust the spice level in this dish to your liking by choosing mild, medium, or spicy Italian sausage at your local grocery store or butcher shop.

PER SERVING: Calories: 414; Total Fat: 13g; Saturated Fat: 4g; Protein: 22g; Total Carbohydrates: 54g; Fiber: 7g; Sugar: 20g; Cholesterol: 34mg

DIY PREP PLANNING

Do you feel like a clean-eating meal-prep extraordinaire yet? If not, the last step in your journey is to learn how to do the meal-prep planning all on your own. Here, we've provided a blank meal planning page for you to work with. Ultimately, it's up to you whether prepping three, four, or five meals fits your lifestyle. The number of meals might also change week to week, depending on your needs.

We hope you use this planner, along with these do's and don'ts, to begin planning your own weekly preps. Remember, stay flexible to ensure the process stays enjoyable—that's how you'll stick to it!

Do

- Utilize the remaining recipes in this book. The have all been designed specifically with clean-eating meal prep in mind and include specific instructions for storing and reheating food. This is the easiest way to get started planning and prepping on your own.

- Pair dishes with complementary ingredients for easy batch cooking. Selecting two chicken recipes to enjoy during the week is a smart move because you can prep the chicken for both recipes in one step. Do this whenever possible to save time.

- Take advantage of clean-eating meal-prep convenience items, like frozen cauliflower rice, frozen cooked brown rice, frozen vegetables, cleaned and cut fresh vegetables, and many others. As long as they don't contain any unwanted or added ingredients, these can be a healthy and time-saving addition to meal preps.

- Alternate cooking methods during your weekly prep. For example, when planning dinners, select a one-pot meal to cook on the stovetop and a sheet-pan meal to cook in the oven. That way, you make the most efficient use of your kitchen and won't have to worry about running out of space or wasting time.

Don't

◆ Prep a recipe you know you won't like. Although we hope you love all these recipes, we totally understand that everyone has their own tastes and preferences. We want you to experiment and get creative, but as you learn what you like, avoid prepping dishes you won't enjoy—you won't eat it later in the week!

◆ Get overwhelmed if your weekly prep schedule doesn't go according to plan. Even if you're only able to prep half the weekly plan, consider it a win—you've still saved yourself time later in the week. Instead of feeling down about the things you didn't do "perfectly," celebrate the victories and learn for next time.

	BREAKFAST	LUNCH	DINNER	SNACK
DAY 1				
DAY 2				
DAY 3				
DAY 4				
DAY 5				

PART THREE

More Clean Recipes to Prep

Welcome to our third and final part of the clean-eating meal-prepping journey. By now, you should be feeling confident in the kitchen, secure in your meal-prep routine, and eager and ready to try out some new recipes. The recipes found in this part of the book are designed to be swapped in and out of your weekly meal-prep routines easily to provide versatility and, of course, delicious meals that help nourish your body. You will find this part broken down into chapters for breakfast prep, snacks and staples prep, smoothies and juices prep, and finally both a plant-based protein prep chapter and an animal-based protein prep chapter so you can prep your meals according to your personal preferences.

Chia Seed Fruit Preserves, page 87

CHAPTER SIX

Staples, Snacks, and Sweet Treats

Homemade Taco Seasoning

MAKES 1 CUP

PREP TIME: 10 minutes

DAIRY-FREE

GLUTEN-FREE

NUT-FREE

SOY-FREE

VEGETARIAN

6 tablespoons
ground cumin

3 tablespoons ground
chili powder

3 tablespoons corn flour

1 tablespoon granulated
garlic

1 tablespoon granulated
onion

1 tablespoon ground
coriander

2 teaspoons paprika

2 teaspoons ground
turmeric

2 teaspoons kosher salt

2 teaspoons freshly ground
black pepper

1 teaspoon ground chipotle
pepper

1 teaspoon ground oregano

½ teaspoon red
pepper flakes

This homemade seasoning, made with your own blend of spices, has no artificial ingredients or unwanted preservatives (which are often hidden in store-bought seasoning blends). Use this seasoning in many of our delicious recipes, like Southwest Breakfast Burritos (page 112) or Chipotle Taco Hummus (page 85).

In a large bowl, whisk the cumin, chili powder, corn flour, granulated garlic, granulated onion, coriander, paprika, turmeric, salt, black pepper, chipotle pepper, oregano, and red pepper flakes until well incorporated. Transfer to a quart-size wide-mouth Mason jar with a tight-fitting lid for convenient storage.

STORAGE: Store in the pantry in an airtight container for up to 3 months.

REUSE TIP: If you have the space in your pantry, make this recipe in double or quadruple batches to keep on hand for many future meal preps.

PER SERVING (1 TABLESPOON): Calories: 25; Total Fat: 1g; Saturated Fat: <1g; Protein: 1g; Total Carbohydrates: 4g; Fiber: 1g; Sugar: <1g; Cholesterol: 0mg

Zesty Lemon Vinaigrette

MAKES 2 CUPS
PREP TIME: 10 minutes

GLUTEN-FREE
NUT-FREE
SOY-FREE
VEGETARIAN

¼ cup freshly squeezed lemon juice

¼ cup white balsamic vinegar

2 tablespoons white wine vinegar

1½ teaspoons sliced scallion, white parts only

1½ teaspoons grated fresh Parmesan

1⅛ teaspoons granulated garlic

1⅛ teaspoons granulated onion

¾ teaspoon sugar

¾ teaspoon salt

½ teaspoon freshly ground black pepper

½ teaspoon Dijon mustard

½ teaspoon minced garlic

⅛ teaspoon red pepper flakes

1½ cups avocado oil

Once you make your own vinaigrette, you'll never go back to store-bought versions. This light, fresh, citrusy vinaigrette is versatile enough to use in a wide variety of recipes in this book, both as a salad dressing and a marinade for meat or plant-based protein. Once you get comfortable making your own vinaigrette at home, try your own flavor combinations using different fruits and vinegars.

1. In a high-speed blender, combine the lemon juice, balsamic vinegar, white wine vinegar, scallions, Parmesan, granulated garlic, granulated onion, sugar, salt, black pepper, Dijon, minced garlic, and red pepper flakes. Blend on high speed until smooth.

2. With the blender still running, slowly drizzle in the oil, allowing it to emulsify.

3. Portion 2 tablespoons of dressing per serving into individual 1½-ounce stainless-steel salad dressing containers as needed for the week and refrigerate.

STORAGE: Refrigerate leftover vinaigrette in a Mason jar, sealed, for up to 2 weeks.

COOKING TIP: If you have an immersion blender, you can blend the ingredients directly in a pint-size (or larger) wide-mouth Mason jar.

PER SERVING (2 TABLESPOONS): Calories: 189; Total Fat: 21g; Saturated Fat: 2g; Protein: <1g; Total Carbohydrates: 2g; Fiber: <1g; Sugar: 1g; Cholesterol: <1mg

Creamy Ranch Dressing

MAKES 1 CUP
PREP TIME: 10 minutes

GLUTEN-FREE

NUT-FREE

SOY-FREE

VEGETARIAN

1 cup full-fat plain
    Greek yogurt
1 tablespoon milk
1 teaspoon white vinegar
1 teaspoon freshly
    squeezed lemon juice
1 teaspoon garlic powder
1 teaspoon onion powder
1 teaspoon dried chives
1 teaspoon dried parsley
½ teaspoon dried dill
½ teaspoon salt
¼ teaspoon freshly ground
    black pepper

This creamy homemade ranch dressing tastes amazing—and unlike preservative-packed store-bought ranch, it's made with ingredients that are actually good for you. Full-fat Greek yogurt is high in protein and contains probiotics that aid digestion and the dried herbs and spices contribute antioxidants and anti-inflammatory properties.

1. In a large bowl, combine the yogurt, milk, vinegar, lemon juice, garlic powder, onion powder, chives, parsley, dill, salt, and pepper. Whisk until all ingredients are incorporated and the mixture is smooth and creamy.

2. Portion 2 tablespoons of dressing per serving into individual 1½-ounce stainless-steel salad dressing containers as needed for the week and refrigerate. Store any remaining dressing for other uses.

STORAGE: Refrigerate leftovers in in a pint-size Mason jar with a tight-fitting lid for up to 2 weeks.

REUSE TIP: Extra dressing can be enjoyed on salads, as a dip, or even used as a marinade for meats.

PER SERVING (2 TABLESPOONS): Calories: 30; Total Fat: 1g; Saturated Fat: 1g; Protein: 3g; Total Carbohydrates: 2g; Fiber: <1g; Sugar: 1g; Cholesterol: 5mg

Chipotle Taco Hummus

SERVES 8
PREP TIME: 15 minutes

DAIRY-FREE

GLUTEN-FREE

NUT-FREE

SOY-FREE

VEGETARIAN

1 (15.5-ounce) can chick-
    peas, drained, liquid
    reserved

2 tablespoons tahini

1 tablespoon freshly
    squeezed lemon juice

2 teaspoons chopped
    chipotle peppers in
    adobo sauce

2 scallions, sliced, white
    and green parts

1 teaspoon minced garlic

½ teaspoon salt

½ teaspoon freshly ground
    black pepper

Cut veggies of choice,
    for serving

Traditional hummus is great, but this taco hummus is even better. Bursting with spices and plenty of plant-based protein, this creamy hummus makes the perfect dip for fresh veggies. Our favorite things to dip in this are bell peppers, baby carrots, and miniature cucumbers.

1. In a food processor or upright blender, combine the chickpeas, tahini, lemon juice, chipotle peppers in adobo, scallions, garlic, salt, and pepper. Puree on high speed for 1 to 1½ minutes, or until completely smooth, stopping halfway through to scrape down the sides, as needed. If the hummus is too thick for your liking, add the reserved chickpea liquid, 1 tablespoon at a time, blending until the hummus reaches your desired consistency (it will thicken once refrigerated).

2. Place ¼-cup portions into each of 5 half-pint Mason jars, seal the lids, and refrigerate. Top with veggies of choice for a quick grab-and-go snack.

STORAGE: Keep refrigerated for up to 5 days.

INGREDIENT TIP: Chipotle peppers in adobo sauce are available (canned) at most grocery stores. If you can't find them or don't have any on hand, use 1 teaspoon of our Homemade Taco Seasoning (page 82), adding more to taste, if desired.

PER SERVING (¼ CUP): Calories: 72; Total Fat: 3g; Saturated Fat: <1g; Protein: 3g; Total Carbohydrates: 9g; Fiber: 3g; Sugar: 2g; Cholesterol: 0mg

Easy Baked Seasoned Chickpeas

SERVES 4
PREP TIME: 10 minutes
COOK TIME: 20 minutes

DAIRY-FREE

GLUTEN-FREE

NUT-FREE

SOY-FREE

VEGETARIAN

1 (15.5-ounce) can chick-
peas, drained and rinsed
1 teaspoon extra-virgin
olive oil
½ teaspoon sea salt
¼ teaspoon cayenne
pepper

These baked chickpeas will become your new favorite snack to prep—almost as easy to prep as they are to eat. When roasted in the oven, chickpeas develop a delightfully crunchy texture, making them a delicious and healthy snacking alternative to potato chips.

1. Preheat the oven to 425°F. Line a baking sheet with foil and set aside.

2. Spread the chickpeas between 2 paper towels and pat dry as thoroughly as possible. Transfer to a large bowl, add the oil, and toss to coat. Stir in the salt and cayenne.

3. Transfer the chickpeas to the prepared baking sheet and spread into a single layer.

4. Place the sheet pan into the oven to bake for 10 minutes. Stir the chickpeas and bake for 10 minutes more, until crispy.

5. Evenly portion into 4 airtight silicone reusable storage bags.

STORAGE: Store in the pantry for up to 7 days.

INGREDIENT TIP: Make this recipe your own by swap-ping in your favorite seasonings, such as garlic powder, Italian seasoning, or cumin.

PER SERVING: Calories: 103; Total Fat: 3g; Saturated Fat: <1g; Protein: 5g; Total Carbohydrates: 15g; Fiber: 4g; Sugar: 3g; Cholesterol: 0mg

Chia Seed Fruit Preserves

MAKES 1 CUP
PREP TIME: 5 minutes
COOK TIME: 25 minutes

DAIRY-FREE
GLUTEN-FREE
NUT-FREE
SOY-FREE
VEGETARIAN

1½ cups fresh blackberries
½ cup water
2 tablespoons honey
1 tablespoon freshly
  squeezed lemon juice
⅛ teaspoon pumpkin
  pie spice
2 tablespoons chia seeds

Fruit and berries provide a delicious antioxidant-rich source of all-natural sweetness. In this recipe, cooking the berries releases their natural sugars and chia seeds provide a natural thickener, making this a healthy, plant-based alternative to store-bought jam or jelly. Try these preserves in a Honey-Berry Yogurt Parfait (page 59) or PB&J Oatmeal Jars (page 108).

1. In a medium saucepan over medium heat, combine the berries, water, honey, lemon juice, and pumpkin pie spice. Bring to a boil, stirring frequently.

2. Stir in the chia seeds, stirring constantly to prevent them from clumping together. Reduce the heat to low and simmer the mixture for 20 minutes, stirring occasionally. Let cool, then transfer to a 1-pint wide-mouth Mason jar with a tight-fitting lid.

STORAGE: Keep refrigerated for up to 2 weeks.

INGREDIENT TIP: Use this recipe to make preserves with nearly any fruit you have on hand—we recommend strawberries or raspberries, but pick what's in season!

PER SERVING (¼ CUP): Calories: 86; Total Fat: 2g; Saturated Fat: 0g; Protein: 2g; Total Carbohydrates: 17g; Fiber: 5g; Sugar: 11g; Cholesterol: 0mg

Chocolate-Banana Chia Seed Pudding

SERVES 4

PREP TIME: 10 minutes, plus 1 hour, or overnight, chilling time

GLUTEN-FREE

NUT-FREE

SOY-FREE

VEGETARIAN

3 cups milk

½ cup chia seeds

1 tablespoon unsweetened cocoa powder

2 teaspoons maple syrup

½ teaspoon pure vanilla extract

2 bananas, sliced

Chia seeds are one of the richest plant-based sources of omega-3 fatty acids and may help reduce inflammation, improve cognition, and reduce high cholesterol levels in the body. When added to liquid, they become gelatinous, creating the perfect pudding-like texture and making this recipe the ideal clean-eating snack or dessert.

1. In a quart-size glass container with an airtight lid, combine the milk, chia seeds, cocoa powder, maple syrup, and vanilla. Seal the lid and shake the mixture vigorously for at least 1 minute to ensure there are no clumps.

2. Evenly portion the pudding into 4 pint-size Mason jars with tight-fitting lids. Top each with banana slices and seal the lids.

3. Refrigerate the jars for at least 1 hour, ideally overnight, to allow them to set.

STORAGE: Keep refrigerated for up to 5 days.

PER SERVING: Calories: 263; Total Fat: 9g; Saturated Fat: 1g; Protein: 11g; Total Carbohydrates: 36g; Fiber: 12g; Sugar: 19g; Cholesterol: 9mg

Chickpea Cookie Dough Bites

SERVES 4

PREP TIME: 20 minutes, plus 5 minutes to chill

> **GLUTEN-FREE**
>
> **SOY-FREE**
>
> **VEGETARIAN**

1 (15.5-ounce) can chickpeas, drained and rinsed

½ cup all-natural peanut butter, smooth or chunky

¼ cup maple syrup

2 tablespoons powdered peanut butter

1 teaspoon vanilla extract

¼ teaspoon salt

¼ cup dark chocolate chips (optional)

The title of this recipe might surprise you, but you'll be shocked at how a can of chickpeas can be transformed into a delicious edible cookie dough packed with plant-based protein. We like to roll this "dough" into energy balls, convenient for grab-and-go snacking, but you can also serve it as a cookie dough dip, enjoyed with fresh strawberries or sliced apples.

1. Place the chickpeas in a food processor or blender and puree on high speed for 30 seconds.

2. Add the peanut butter, maple syrup, powdered peanut butter, vanilla, and salt. Puree until smooth, scraping down the sides as needed. Transfer the mixture to a medium bowl and gently fold in the chocolate chips (if using).

3. Refrigerate the mixture for 5 minutes to chill. Roll into 16 (1-inch) balls.

4. Portion 4 cookie dough bites into each of 4 silicone reusable storage bags.

STORAGE: Keep refrigerated for up to 5 days.

INGREDIENT TIP: Use any type of nut (almond, cashew) or seed butter (sunflower, hemp) in place of the peanut butter to accommodate for allergies and taste preferences.

PER SERVING (4 BALLS): Calories: 347; Total Fat: 18g; Saturated Fat: 3g; Protein: 14g; Total Carbohydrates: 36g; Fiber: 7g; Sugar: 17g; Cholesterol: 0mg

Ransom's Berry-Mint Nice Cream

SERVES 4

PREP TIME: 15 minutes, plus 1 hour or overnight to freeze

DAIRY-FREE
GLUTEN-FREE
NUT-FREE
SOY-FREE
VEGETARIAN

3 bananas

1 pint fresh blackberries

½ teaspoon chopped fresh mint

1 (13.5-ounce) can full-fat unsweetened coconut milk

1 (15-ounce) can coconut cream

⅛ teaspoon vanilla extract

This recipe was inspired by our 5-year old son, Ransom, who loves to pick blackberries and mint from our garden. Made with creamy coconut milk and coconut cream, this easy, no-churn ice cream alternative is perfectly suited to the clean-eating lifestyle.

1. In a food processor or blender, combine the bananas, blackberries, and mint. Pulse or blend for three 15-second intervals.

2. Add the coconut milk, coconut cream, and vanilla. Pulse or blend on high speed for 1 to 1½ minutes, or until smooth, scraping down the sides as needed.

3. Evenly portion 1-cup servings into 4 airtight freezer-safe containers or ice pop molds. Transfer any leftover ice cream to another airtight freezer-safe container. Freeze for at least 1 hour, or ideally overnight, to set.

STORAGE: Keep frozen for up to 2 months.

INGREDIENT TIP: Vary this recipe using different types of berries, depending on what is in season. (If nothing is in season, frozen berries work great, too.)

PER SERVING: Calories: 522; Total Fat: 44g; Saturated Fat: 39g; Protein: 5g; Total Carbohydrates: 31g; Fiber: 6g; Sugar: 19g; Cholesterol: 0mg

Raspberry-Peach Smoothie, page 95

CHAPTER SEVEN

Smoothies and Juices

Anti-Inflammatory CBD Smoothie

SERVES 2

PREP TIME: 5 minutes

GLUTEN-FREE

NUT-FREE

SOY-FREE

VEGETARIAN

1 cup frozen mango chunks

1 cup frozen pineapple chunks

1 cup packed fresh spinach

1 cup milk

1 tablespoon hemp seeds

1 mL CBD hemp oil

This tropical fruit smoothie brings the health benefits of its plant-based ingredients to a new level with the addition of anti-inflammatory CBD hemp oil and hemp seeds. CBD hemp oil is a great supplement for a clean-eating lifestyle and blends perfectly with the flavors of this drink.

1. In a high-speed blender, combine the mango, pineapple, spinach, milk, hemp seeds, and CBD oil. Blend on high speed for 2 minutes, or until completely smooth, scraping down the sides as needed.

2. Evenly portion into 2 pint-size Mason jars with tight-fitting lids.

STORAGE: Refrigerate for up to 5 days. Shake well before enjoying.

INGREDIENT TIP: New to using CBD hemp oil as a supplement? Be sure to reference our Clean Eating + CBD Guide in the Resources section (page 166).

PER SERVING: Calories: 162; Total Fat: 4g; Saturated Fat: 1g; Protein: 7g; Total Carbohydrates: 27g; Fiber: 3g; Sugar: 23g; Cholesterol: 6mg

Raspberry-Peach Smoothie

SERVES 2

PREP TIME: 5 minutes

GLUTEN-FREE

NUT-FREE

SOY-FREE

VEGETARIAN

1 peach, pitted and cut
into slices

1 cup fresh raspberries

1 cup ice

¾ cup milk

¼ cup full-fat plain
Greek yogurt

1 tablespoon honey

1 tablespoon ground flax

½ teaspoon ground
turmeric

¼ teaspoon ground
cinnamon

¼ teaspoon vanilla extract

This delicious, refreshing smoothie is the perfect combination of tart and sweet, and it's filled with antioxidant-rich ingredients such as ground flax, turmeric, and cinnamon. The ingredients of this smoothie provide prebiotics and probiotics, which are both important for good gut health and digestion.

1. In a high-speed blender, combine the peach slices, raspberries, ice, milk, yogurt, honey, flax, turmeric, cinnamon, and vanilla. Blend on high speed for 2 minutes, or until completely smooth, scraping down the sides as needed.

2. Evenly portion into 2 pint-size Mason jars with tight-fitting lids.

STORAGE: Keep refrigerated for up to 5 days. Shake well before enjoying.

INGREDIENT TIP: If you don't have ground flax, use chia seeds.

PER SERVING: Calories: 180; Total Fat: 4g; Saturated Fat: 2g; Protein: 8g; Total Carbohydrates: 31g; Fiber: 6g; Sugar: 24g; Cholesterol: 9mg

Creamy Cocoa-Mint Smoothie

SERVES 2
PREP TIME: 5 minutes

GLUTEN-FREE

NUT-FREE

SOY-FREE

VEGETARIAN

2 bananas
1 cup lightly packed
   fresh spinach
1 cup ice
¾ cup milk
¼ cup full-fat plain
   Greek yogurt
1 tablespoon cocoa powder
1 teaspoon chopped
   fresh mint
¼ teaspoon vanilla extract

Creamy, minty, and chocolatey, this smoothie makes a decadent yet refreshing breakfast, snack, or even dessert. The bananas provide a light, creamy base and the cocoa powder and mint complement one another perfectly to create a clean-eating treat that will likely become a favorite.

1. In a high-speed blender, combine the bananas, spinach, ice, milk, yogurt, cocoa powder, mint, and vanilla. Blend on high speed for 2 minutes, or until completely smooth, scraping down the sides as needed.

2. Evenly portion into 2 pint-size Mason jars with tight-fitting lids.

STORAGE: Keep refrigerated for up to 5 days. Shake well before enjoying.

SUBSTITUTION TIP: If you don't have fresh mint, use ¼ teaspoon mint extract or food-grade peppermint essential oil.

PER SERVING: Calories: 181; Total Fat: 3g; Saturated Fat: 2g; Protein: 8g; Total Carbohydrates: 35g; Fiber: 4g; Sugar: 20g; Cholesterol: 9mg

Super Green Detox Juice

SERVES 2

PREP TIME: 5 minutes

DAIRY-FREE

GLUTEN-FREE

NUT-FREE

SOY-FREE

VEGETARIAN

1 cup packed fresh spinach

1 cup packed baby kale

2 green apples, cored

2 celery stalks

½ lemon, peeled
   and seeded

½ teaspoon grated
   lemon zest

1 (½-inch) piece fresh
   ginger, peeled

Feeling less than great? Looking for a little pick-me-up? This juice is for you. Made with an array of super-nutritious ingredients, this vibrant green juice tastes amazing. We like to drink it to feel better when we're under the weather. Maybe it will help you feel better, too!

1. Slowly add the spinach, kale, apples, celery, lemon, lemon zest, and ginger to a juicer.

2. Evenly portion into 2 pint-size Mason jars with tight-fitting lids.

STORAGE: Keep refrigerated for up to 5 days. Shake well before enjoying.

INGREDIENT TIP: You can use spinach and kale interchangeably here, or use other dark-green leafy vegetables, depending on what you have on hand or what is in season.

PER SERVING: Calories: 111; Total Fat: 1g; Saturated Fat: <1g; Protein: 2g; Total Carbohydrates: 29g; Fiber: 6g; Sugar: 20g; Cholesterol: 0mg

Citrus-Coconut Rehydration Drink

SERVES 2
PREP TIME: 5 minutes

DAIRY-FREE

GLUTEN-FREE

NUT-FREE

SOY-FREE

VEGETARIAN

1 small cucumber

1 orange

1 lemon

½ cup packed fresh spinach

1 (½-inch) piece fresh
    ginger, peeled

¼ teaspoon salt

¼ teaspoon sugar

⅛ teaspoon ground cayenne
    pepper

2 cups coconut water

We designed this refreshing and rehydrating drink to provide a source of electrolytes, which we lose when we sweat during physical activity. Our homemade version of a sports drink, it is made with no artificial ingredients or sugars and is perfect for a clean-eating lifestyle.

1. Slowly add the cucumber, orange, lemon, spinach, ginger, salt, sugar, and cayenne to a juicer.

2. Evenly portion the juice mixture into 2 pint-size Mason jars with tight-fitting lids. Pour 1 cup of coconut water into each jar and seal the lids.

STORAGE: Keep refrigerated for up to 5 days. Shake well before enjoying.

INGREDIENT TIP: For a dressed-up version of this drink, for each serving, pour in half a 12-ounce can of zero-calorie sparkling water just before enjoying.

PER SERVING: Calories: 101; Total Fat: 1g; Saturated Fat: 1g; Protein: 3g; Total Carbohydrates: 23g; Fiber: 6g; Sugar: 15g; Cholesterol: 0mg

Strawberry-Watermelon Lemonade

SERVES 2
PREP TIME: 5 minutes

DAIRY-FREE
GLUTEN-FREE
NUT-FREE
SOY-FREE
VEGETARIAN

1 cup fresh strawberries, stemmed

1½ cups diced seedless watermelon

¼ cup freshly squeezed lemon juice

1 tablespoon honey

We're willing to bet this drink will become your new favorite treat for summertime. Made in a blender instead of a juicer, this lemonade retains all the important dietary fiber from the strawberries and watermelon but is still light enough to sip on all day long.

1. In a high-speed blender, combine the strawberries, watermelon, lemon juice, and honey. Blend on high speed for 2 minutes, or until completely pureed.

2. Evenly portion into 2 pint-size Mason jars with tight-fitting lids.

STORAGE: Keep refrigerated for up to 5 days. Shake well before enjoying.

INGREDIENT TIP: If you have fresh lemons available, we strongly recommend using freshly squeezed lemon juice.

PER SERVING: Calories: 85; Total Fat: <1g; Saturated Fat: 0g; Protein: 1g; Total Carbohydrates: 22g; Fiber: 2g; Sugar: 18g; Cholesterol: 0mg

Hemp Seed Milk

SERVES 4

PREP TIME: 5 minutes, plus 20 minutes to soak

DAIRY-FREE

GLUTEN-FREE

NUT-FREE

SOY-FREE

VEGETARIAN

1 cup hulled hemp seeds
4 cups water
1 teaspoon maple syrup
½ teaspoon vanilla extract
¼ teaspoon salt

Whether you are dairy-free for health reasons or simply looking to incorporate more plants into your diet, hemp seed milk is a nutritious dairy-free alternative milk that is easy to make at home. Unlike harder nuts and seeds that require overnight soaking, hemp seeds are soft and only need to soak for 20 minutes before you can blend them up into a creamy, delicious plant milk.

1. In a high-speed blender, combine the hemp seeds and water. Let soak for 20 minutes.

2. Blend the mixture on high speed for 1 minute.

3. Add the maple syrup, vanilla, and salt. Blend on high speed for 30 seconds.

4. If you prefer super-smooth milk, strain the mixture through a fine-mesh sieve, nut milk bag, or cheesecloth set over a bowl.

5. Evenly portion into 4 half-pint Mason jars with tight-fitting lids.

STORAGE: Keep refrigerated for up to 5 days. Shake well before enjoying.

SUBSTITUTION TIP: To make unsweetened hemp milk, especially for savory cooking, omit the maple syrup and vanilla extract.

PER SERVING: Calories: 226; Total Fat: 20g; Saturated Fat: 2g; Protein: 13g; Total Carbohydrates: 5g; Fiber: 2g; Sugar: 2g; Cholesterol: 0mg

Nonalcoholic Fruit Sangria

SERVES 4
PREP TIME: 5 minutes,
plus 12 hours to chill

DAIRY-FREE
GLUTEN-FREE
NUT-FREE
SOY-FREE
VEGETARIAN

1 orange, washed with
 rind on, cut into slices
 and diced
1 lemon, washed with
 rind on, cut into slices
 and diced
4 cups no-sugar-added red
 grape juice
1½ cups frozen berry mix
1 (3-inch) cinnamon stick

You can absolutely enjoy alcohol in moderation as part of a clean-eating lifestyle—though this sangria is delicious without any alcohol added. This nonalcoholic, no-sugar-added version is a festive summery treat. To make an alcoholic version, use 1 cup red grape juice and pour in a bottle (750 ml) of your favorite sweet red wine, like merlot or pinot noir.

1. In a half gallon–size Mason jar with a tight-fitting lid, muddle the orange and lemon with a wooden spoon.

2. Pour in the grape juice and add the frozen berries and cinnamon stick. Seal the lid and refrigerate for 12 hours for the flavors to develop.

3. Strain the mixture into 4 pint-size Mason jars with tight-fitting lids.

STORAGE: Keep refrigerated for up to 5 days. Shake well before enjoying.

SUBSTITUTION TIP: To make a white sangria, swap the red grape juice for white grape juice and swap the berries for frozen peaches and pineapples.

PER SERVING: Calories: 205; Total Fat: <1g; Saturated Fat: 0g; Protein: 1g; Total Carbohydrates: 52g; Fiber: 2g; Sugar: 47g; Cholesterol: 0mg

High-Protein Breakfast Box, page 116

CHAPTER EIGHT

Breakfast

Chocolate-Cherry Granola Bars

SERVES 8
PREP TIME: 20 minutes,
plus 1 hour to cool
COOK TIME: 10 minutes

2 cups rolled oats
1 cup sliced or slivered
    almonds
1 cup unsweetened
    coconut flakes
1 cup pitted dates
½ cup almond butter
¼ cup honey
2 tablespoons coconut oil
1 tablespoon vanilla extract
½ cup dark chocolate chips
½ cup unsweetened dried
    cherries
½ teaspoon sea salt

These delicious granola bars are an ideal grab-and-go breakfast option for busy mornings and make a satisfying snack. Made with simple whole-food ingredients, these sweet bars combine the delicious flavors of sweet cherries and almonds with dark chocolate chips for a delicious breakfast to go.

1. Preheat the oven to 400°F. Line a large baking sheet with foil. Line an 8-by-8-inch glass baking dish with parchment paper and set aside.

2. Spread the oats and almonds in an even layer on the prepared baking sheet.

3. Place in the oven and toast for 6 minutes. Remove the baking sheet from the oven and add the coconut flakes. Return to the oven and toast for 2 minutes more, until all ingredients are golden brown but not burnt. Set aside to cool.

4. In a food processor, pulse the dates on high speed to form a thick paste. Transfer the pureed dates to a small saucepan and place it over medium heat. Stir in the almond butter, honey, and coconut oil. Cook for 2 to 3 minutes, until all ingredients are well incorporated. Remove from the heat and stir in the vanilla.

5. In a large bowl, combine the date mixture and the cooled oat mixture. Add the chocolate chips and dried cherries and mix well with a spatula until all ingredients are well combined. Transfer the mixture to the prepared baking dish and press it into an even layer, spreading it to the corners of the dish. Sprinkle with salt and refrigerate for at least 1 hour to set.

6. Cut the mixture into 8 equal-size granola bars. Tightly wrap individual granola bars in a layer of parchment followed by a layer of plastic wrap.

STORAGE: Keep refrigerated for up to 5 days, or freeze for up to 3 months. Thaw in the refrigerator overnight.

SUBSTITUTION TIP: Swap the types of nuts, nut butters, and unsweetened dried fruits for unlimited flavor combinations for future meal preps.

PER SERVING: Calories: 531; Total Fat: 30g; Saturated Fat: 12g; Protein: 11g; Total Carbohydrates: 59g; Fiber: 10g; Sugar: 32g; Cholesterol: 1mg

Apple-Cinnamon Oatmeal Cake

SERVES 4
PREP TIME: 15 minutes
COOK TIME: 45 minutes

GLUTEN-FREE
SOY-FREE

Nonstick cooking spray
2 ripe bananas
2 large eggs
1¼ cups milk
¼ cup loosely packed light
  brown sugar
1 tablespoon chia seeds
1 tablespoon ground
  cinnamon
1 teaspoon baking powder
½ teaspoon salt
½ teaspoon ground nutmeg
2 cups old-fashioned
  rolled oats
½ cup crushed walnuts
1 red apple, thinly sliced
2 cups sliced fresh
  strawberries

Made with fiber-rich rolled oats, heart-healthy walnuts, and naturally sweet bananas, this cake makes a lightly sweet but nutrient-dense breakfast to keep you fueled through the morning. We serve this cake with a side of fresh fruit, but for a higher-protein breakfast, swap the fruit for hard-boiled eggs.

1. Preheat the oven to 400°F. Coat a 9-by-9-inch glass baking dish with cooking spray. Set aside.

2. In a high-speed blender, combine the bananas, eggs, milk, brown sugar, chia seeds, cinnamon, baking powder, salt, and nutmeg. Blend on high speed in 30-second intervals until smooth, scraping down the sides as needed.

3. Place the oats in a large bowl. Pour the blender mixture over the oats and stir until fully incorporated. Transfer the batter to the prepared baking dish and top with the walnuts and apple slices.

4. Bake for 45 minutes, or until golden brown and a toothpick inserted into the center comes out clean. Set aside to cool. Once cooled, cut into 8 slices.

5. Portion 2 slices of cake into the bigger side of 4 large two-compartment glass meal-prep containers with tight-fitting lids. Fill the adjacent compartment with the strawberries. Cover and refrigerate.

STORAGE: Keep refrigerated for up to 5 days. The oatmeal cake can be enjoyed cold, at room temperature, or warm. To reheat, microwave the cake on high power for 30 seconds to 1 minute. Leftover cake can be frozen in an airtight container for up to 2 months. Thaw in the refrigerator overnight.

PER SERVING: Calories: 456; Total Fat: 14g; Saturated Fat: 3g; Protein: 14g; Total Carbohydrates: 75g; Fiber: 11g; Sugar: 35g; Cholesterol: 86mg

PB&J Oatmeal Jars

SERVES 4
PREP TIME: 10 minutes
COOK TIME: 10 minutes

GLUTEN-FREE

SOY-FREE

VEGETARIAN

4 tablespoons Chia Seed Fruit Preserves (page 87)

2 cups quick cooking oats

4 cups milk

1 tablespoon honey

1 teaspoon chia seeds

4 tablespoons almond butter

These oatmeal jars combine the nostalgic childhood flavor of PB&J with healthy-for-you ingredients like oatmeal, chia seeds, fruits, and nuts. This recipe is ultra-versatile—you can repurpose this basic formula into countless variations, switching out the type of nut butter and preserves to your liking.

1. If needed, prepare the preserves.

2. In a medium saucepan, combine the oats and milk and cook the oats according to the package directions for stovetop preparation.

3. Stir in the honey and chia seeds.

4. Evenly portion the oatmeal into 4 pint-size Mason jars with tight-fitting lids. Top each serving with 1 tablespoon of almond butter and 1 tablespoon of preserves. Seal the lids and refrigerate.

STORAGE: Keep refrigerated for up to 5 days. The mixture will continue to thicken with time, so stir in hot water, 1 tablespoon at a time, to thin the oats as needed.

INGREDIENT TIP: If you don't have any preserves prepared, use your favorite store-bought jam—just be sure to check the ingredients to ensure there are no added sugars, additives, or artificial preservatives.

PER SERVING: Calories: 395; Total Fat: 15g; Saturated Fat: 3g; Protein: 18g; Total Carbohydrates: 52g; Fiber: 8g; Sugar: 21g; Cholesterol: 12mg

Sweet Berry Quinoa Bowls

SERVES 4
PREP TIME: 5 minutes
COOK TIME: 30 minutes

GLUTEN-FREE

SOY-FREE

VEGETARIAN

2 cups dried quinoa, rinsed
4 cups milk
1 tablespoon maple syrup
½ teaspoon vanilla extract
½ cup fresh or frozen
    raspberries
½ cup fresh or frozen
    blackberries
¼ cup almonds

You may be more accustomed to seeing quinoa used in savory lunch and dinner recipes but it also makes a delicious alternative to oatmeal at breakfast. Prepared with creamy milk, maple syrup, and fresh or frozen berries, this naturally sweet plant-based breakfast bowl will keep you full and energized throughout the morning.

1. In a medium saucepan, combine the quinoa and milk. Cook the quinoa according to the package directions for stovetop preparation.

2. Stir in the maple syrup and vanilla. Evenly portion the quinoa into 4 pint-size Mason jars with tight-fitting lids. Top each serving with 2 tablespoons of raspberries, 2 tablespoons of blackberries, and 1 tablespoon of almonds. Seal the lids and refrigerate.

STORAGE: Keep refrigerated for up to 5 days. Enjoy cold or warm. To reheat, remove the lid and microwave on high power for 1 to 1½ minutes.

INGREDIENT TIP: Swap the berries and almonds for any fruit and nuts you have on hand or whatever's in season.

PER SERVING: Calories: 506; Total Fat: 12g; Saturated Fat: 3g; Protein: 23g; Total Carbohydrates: 79g; Fiber: 9g; Sugar: 25g; Cholesterol: 12mg

Sausage & Spinach Quesadillas

SERVES 4
PREP TIME: 10 minutes
COOK TIME: 40 minutes

NUT-FREE

SOY-FREE

8 ounces fresh ground
   breakfast sausage
8 ounces fresh baby
   spinach, stemmed
1 teaspoon butter
4 large eggs, beaten
4 (10-inch) whole-wheat
   tortillas
1 cup shredded Monterey
   Jack cheese, divided
2 cups sliced fruit or
   vegetables of choice

These delicious breakfast quesadillas offer a serving of vegetables, protein, fat, and complex carbohydrates, making them a well-rounded meal-prepped start to your day. Get creative by switching out the veggies and meat in this recipe— it's a great way to use up leftovers from last week's meal prep.

1. In a large skillet over medium-high heat, brown the ground sausage for 4 or 5 minutes, stirring frequently and breaking up large chunks of meat until it's cooked about halfway through.

2. Add half the spinach. Cook for 2 to 3 minutes to cook it down, stirring frequently. Add the remaining spinach and repeat.

3. Using a spatula, push the sausage and spinach to the outer edges of the skillet. Add the butter to the center of the skillet and let it melt until it bubbles.

4. Add the eggs to the center of the skillet and cook for 1 to 2 minutes, stirring occasionally, until halfway cooked.

5. Stir the sausage and spinach into the eggs and continue cooking until the eggs are done to your liking. Transfer the mixture to a large bowl. Set aside. Clean the skillet and place it over medium heat.

6. Once hot, place a tortilla in the skillet and sprinkle it evenly with ¼ cup of cheese. Add one-fourth of the egg mixture to one side of the tortilla. Cook until the cheese on the other side of the tortilla begins to melt, then fold it over onto the egg side. Press down firmly with the back of a spatula so it sticks. Cook for 1 or 2 minutes per side, until golden brown on both sides. Remove from the skillet. Repeat with the remaining ingredients to make 3 more quesadillas.

7. Slice each quesadilla into 4 wedges. Portion 4 wedges into one side of 4 large two-compartment glass meal-prep containers. Fill the adjacent compartment with ½ cup of sliced fruit or vegetables. Cover and refrigerate.

STORAGE: Keep refrigerated for up to 5 days. Reheat the quesadillas in the microwave on high power for 1½ to 2 minutes just before eating.

COOKING TIP: If you find your quesadillas are sticking to the skillet, coat the skillet with cooking spray before cooking each quesadilla.

PER SERVING: Calories: 577; Total Fat: 36g; Saturated Fat: 15g; Protein: 29g; Total Carbohydrates: 38g; Fiber: 7g; Sugar: 5g; Cholesterol: 249mg

Southwest Breakfast Burritos

SERVES 4
PREP TIME: 20 minutes
COOK TIME: 10 minutes

NUT-FREE

SOY-FREE

2 tablespoons Homemade
Taco Seasoning (page 82)

6 large eggs

1 tablespoon butter

¼ cup sliced (⅛ inch)
scallion, white and
green parts

1 (15-ounce) can black
beans, drained
and rinsed

4 (10-inch) whole-wheat
tortillas

1 cup shredded Cheddar
cheese, divided

These hearty breakfast burritos are exactly what you want to stock in your clean-eating freezer. Quick to put together, convenient to eat on the go, and delicious, we recommend making a double or triple batch to keep frozen. That way, on super-busy mornings, you can rest assured knowing you have a clean-eating breakfast ready and waiting.

1. If needed, prepare the taco seasoning.

2. In a medium bowl, whisk the taco seasoning and eggs for 1 to 2 minutes until well combined. Set aside.

3. In a large skillet over medium-high heat, melt the butter until it bubbles. Add the scallions and cook for 2 to 3 minutes, until tender.

4. Add the black beans and cook for 1 minute, until heated through. Using a spatula, push the bean and scallion mixture to the outer edges of the skillet.

5. Add the eggs to the center of the skillet and cook for 1 to 2 minutes, stirring occasionally, until cooked halfway through.

6. Stir the beans and scallions into the eggs and cook until the eggs are done to your liking. Remove the skillet from the heat.

7. Place the tortillas on a flat surface and sprinkle the middle of each with ¼ cup of Cheddar cheese. Spread one-fourth of the egg mixture across the center of each tortilla.

8. Roll the burritos: Fold the edge of the tortilla closest to you over the filling. Using your fingertips, tuck the edge under the filling and pull the tortilla back toward you, pushing the filling into a cylinder. Fold in the left and right sides to seal the ends. Then, tightly roll the tortilla away from you into a burrito.

9. Tightly wrap individual burritos in parchment paper followed by plastic wrap.

STORAGE: Keep refrigerated for up to 5 days, or freeze for up to 3 months. Thaw in the refrigerator overnight. To reheat, remove the wrapper and microwave the burrito on high power for 1½ minutes, or until heated through.

COOKING TIP: Warm tortillas are easier to wrap than cold tortillas and less likely to tear. We suggest removing your tortillas from the refrigerator while you cook so by the time you're ready to roll the burritos, they'll have reached room temperature.

PER SERVING: Calories: 545; Total Fat: 26g; Saturated Fat: 11g; Protein: 28g; Total Carbohydrates: 55g; Fiber: 14g; Sugar: 4g; Cholesterol: 315mg

Bacon, Egg & Cheese Cups

SERVES 4
PREP TIME: 10 minutes
COOK TIME: 20 minutes

GLUTEN-FREE
NUT-FREE
SOY-FREE

8 large eggs
¼ cup milk
½ teaspoon salt
¼ teaspoon freshly ground
 black pepper
4 uncured bacon slices, cut
 into ½-inch pieces
8 teaspoons shredded
 Cheddar cheese, divided
2 cups sliced fruit or
 vegetables of choice

These simple and convenient egg cups are likely to become a staple of your meal-prep routine. They're easy to customize with your favorite vegetables and protein fillings and even easier to prep for a true grab-and-go breakfast. This is another great recipe to double, as these egg cups can be frozen for up to 3 months (see Storage tip).

1. Preheat the oven to 400°F. Line a large baking sheet with foil and set aside.

2. In a medium bowl, whisk the eggs, milk, salt, and pepper for 1 to 2 minutes until well combined. Set aside.

3. In a medium skillet over medium heat, cook the bacon to your preferred doneness. Remove the bacon from the pan and set aside, leaving the bacon fat in the pan.

4. Using a silicone basting brush, generously brush the bacon fat into 8 cups of a standard muffin tin, coating the edges and bottoms thoroughly to prevent sticking.

5. Evenly distribute the egg mixture among the 8 prepared muffin cups. Add 1 teaspoon of cheese to each. Portion the cut bacon evenly into the 8 cups. Gently stir each cup to incorporate the cheese and bacon.

6. Place the muffin tin on top of the prepared baking sheet to catch any spillage and carefully place the baking sheet with the muffin tin in the oven. Bake for 15 minutes, or until the eggs are set in the center. Remove from the oven and set aside to cool for 10 minutes. (This is a great time to slice the fruit and vegetables for serving.)

7. Use a spoon to scoop the egg cups out of the muffin tins. If they're sticking, run a knife around the edges of each cup to loosen.

8. Portion 2 egg muffins into the larger compartments of 4 large two-compartment glass meal-prep containers. Add ½ cup of sliced fruit or vegetables to the adjacent compartment. Cover and refrigerate.

STORAGE: Keep refrigerated for up to 5 days. To freeze, wrap individual egg cups in parchment paper followed by plastic wrap and place in an airtight freezer-safe container. Keep frozen for up to 3 months. Thaw in the refrigerator overnight. To reheat, remove the wrappers and microwave on high power for about 45 seconds, or until warmed through.

COOKING TIP: For an added serving of vegetables, add fresh or frozen cooked chopped vegetables to the muffin cups during step 5.

PER SERVING: Calories: 245; Total Fat: 16g; Saturated Fat: 5g; Protein: 17g; Total Carbohydrates: 8g; Fiber: 2g; Sugar: 6g; Cholesterol: 387mg

High-Protein Breakfast Box

SERVES 4
PREP TIME: 15 minutes

GLUTEN-FREE

SOY-FREE

2 cups full-fat plain
    Greek yogurt
1 cup fresh blueberries
1 cup sliced fresh
    strawberries
1 cup granola
8 large hard-boiled eggs,
    peeled (see Cooking tip)
½ cup almonds, divided

This highly customizable breakfast box is quick to assemble, making it perfect for meal preps when you're crunched for time. Greek yogurt and hard-boiled eggs provide protein and the fruit and granola offer plenty of complex carbohydrates, making this balanced breakfast an ideal meal to enjoy after a morning workout.

1. Portion ½ cup of yogurt into the largest compartment of 4 large three-compartment glass meal-prep containers. Top the yogurt in each container with ¼ cup of blueberries, ¼ cup of strawberries, and ¼ cup of granola.

2. Place 2 hard-boiled eggs in one of the small compartments of each container.

3. Portion 2 tablespoons of almonds into the other small compartment of each container. Cover and refrigerate.

STORAGE: Keep refrigerated for up to 5 days.

COOKING TIP: To save time making hard-boiled eggs, look for precooked peeled eggs at the grocery store. Alternatively, prepare large batches of hard-boiled eggs and keep them refrigerated for up to 1 week. To prepare hard-boiled eggs, in a medium saucepan, combine the eggs with enough water to cover by 1 inch and bring to a boil. Once boiling, turn off the heat and let the eggs rest on the still-hot burner for 10 to 12 minutes before letting cool and peeling.

PER SERVING: Calories: 488; Total Fat: 25g; Saturated Fat: 7g; Protein: 29g; Total Carbohydrates: 39g; Fiber: 7g; Sugar: 15g; Cholesterol: 347mg

Homemade Breakfast Sandwiches

SERVES 4
PREP TIME: 5 minutes
COOK TIME: 15 minutes

NUT-FREE

SOY-FREE

4 whole-wheat English
    muffins, split
1 teaspoon butter
4 large eggs
1 (7-ounce) package
    uncured ham (8 slices)
4 slices Cheddar cheese

These Homemade Breakfast Sandwiches are another great recipe to make in a double or triple batch to store in the freezer for busy days when you don't have time to do a full meal prep (see storage instructions). For an added serving of veggies, add 1 cup of spinach right into your eggs, or sauté the spinach separately and add it on top of the ham, before the cheese.

1. Lightly toast the English muffins, until barely browned. Set aside.

2. In a large skillet with a lid over medium-high heat, melt the butter until it bubbles. Crack the eggs into the skillet and fry them to your preference. (We recommend cooking them over-hard so the yolk doesn't make a mess.)

3. Turn the heat to low and top each egg with 2 slices of ham and 1 slice of cheese. Cover the skillet and cook for 1 minute more, so the cheese begins to melt. Remove from the heat.

4. Place each egg, ham, and cheese stack between the halves of the toasted English muffins. Tightly wrap individual sandwiches in parchment paper followed by plastic wrap.

STORAGE: Keep refrigerated for up to 5 days, or freeze for up to 3 months. Thaw in the refrigerator overnight. To reheat, remove the wrapper and microwave on high power for 1½ minutes, or until warmed through.

PER SERVING: Calories: 357; Total Fat: 16g; Saturated Fat: 7g; Protein: 26g; Total Carbohydrates: 29g; Fiber: 4g; Sugar: 6g; Cholesterol: 218mg

Healthy Crustless Veggie Quiche

SERVES 4
PREP TIME: 15 minutes
COOK TIME: About 1 hour

> **GLUTEN-FREE**
> **NUT-FREE**
> **SOY-FREE**

1 tablespoon butter, at room temperature
¼ cup grated Parmesan
1 tablespoon extra-virgin olive oil
½ cup diced (½ inch) white onion
1 teaspoon salt, divided
1 cup diced (½ inch) white mushrooms
1 cup fresh spinach, chopped
1 tablespoon minced garlic
8 large eggs
1 cup milk
1 teaspoon ground turmeric
½ teaspoon freshly ground black pepper
8 blanched asparagus spears

This easy-but-fancy Parmesan-crusted quiche is quick to make and a delicious way to make use of a large batch of farm-fresh eggs, if you're lucky enough to have them. We find ourselves making this quiche repeatedly—it's a super-satisfying breakfast, lunch, or dinner and it's a convenient to repurpose leftover raw or cooked veggies hanging around in the refrigerator.

1. Adjust an oven rack to the center position and preheat the oven to 400°F. Coat a 9-inch glass pie dish with butter.

2. Sprinkle the Parmesan into the prepared pie dish and gently shake it to form a light, even coating across the bottom and sides. Set aside.

3. Place a medium skillet over medium heat and add the oil, onion, and ½ teaspoon of salt. Sauté for 2 minutes, stirring frequently, until the onion is translucent. Add the mushrooms, spinach, and garlic. Cook for 3 to 4 minutes, until the vegetables are softened. Remove from the heat.

4. Crack the eggs into a large bowl. Add the milk, turmeric, pepper, and remaining ½ teaspoon of salt. Whisk until fully incorporated. Ladle the egg mixture into the pie dish until it is halfway full. Carefully add the vegetable mixture to the dish. Ladle the remaining eggs on top of the vegetables.

5. Arrange the asparagus on top of the quiche—feel free to make it pretty!

6. Gently place the quiche in the center of the oven, being careful not to spill it. Bake for 45 to 55 minutes, or until the top is golden brown and the internal temperature reaches 165°F. Remove from the oven and let cool. Cut the cooled quiche into 8 wedges.

7. Portion 2 slices of quiche into each of 4 large single-compartment glass meal-prep containers with tight-fitting lids. Cover and refrigerate.

STORAGE: Keep refrigerated for up to 5 days. Reheat individual portions in the microwave on high power for 1½ to 2 minutes just before eating.

INGREDIENT TIP: If you have leftover cooked vegetables at the end of the week, dice them and throw them in—this quiche recipe is a great way to give them new life (plus, it saves money and time).

PER SERVING: Calories: 272; Total Fat: 18g; Saturated Fat: 7g; Protein: 17g; Total Carbohydrates: 11g; Fiber: 2g; Sugar: 6g; Cholesterol: 344mg

Red Pepper Shakshuka (Eggs in Tomato Sauce)

SERVES 4
PREP TIME: 10 minutes
COOK TIME: 25 minutes

DAIRY-FREE

GLUTEN-FREE

NUT-FREE

SOY-FREE

1 tablespoon extra-virgin olive oil

1 small yellow onion, diced

1 medium red bell pepper, cut into thin strips

2 garlic cloves, minced

2 cups chopped kale

1 tablespoon red wine vinegar

1 teaspoon Italian seasoning

½ teaspoon freshly ground black pepper

¼ teaspoon red pepper flakes (optional)

¼ teaspoon salt

1 (28-ounce) can no-salt-added diced tomatoes with juice

8 large eggs

Shakshuka, a dish made with eggs cooked in tomato-and-pepper sauce, has origins in North African and Mediterranean cuisines. It fits beautifully into a clean-eating meal plan, offering a high-protein, low-carb breakfast that is both hearty and healthy. Our version uses kale and Italian seasoning, but feel free to swap seasonings to taste—traditional seasonings include cumin, paprika, and cayenne pepper.

1. In a large cast-iron or nonstick skillet with a lid over medium heat, heat the oil. Add the onion and cook for 2 to 3 minutes, stirring frequently, until translucent.

2. Add the red bell pepper and cook for 5 minutes, stirring frequently, until the pepper and onion are soft.

3. Stir in the garlic.

4. One handful at a time, add the kale. Cook, stirring continuously, adding more kale as it wilts.

5. Pour in the vinegar and deglaze the pan, stirring constantly for 1 minute to remove any stuck bits from the bottom.

6. Add the Italian seasoning, black pepper, red pepper flakes (if using), and salt. Stir to incorporate.

7. Add the diced tomatoes and their juices and stir to fully incorporate. Cover the skillet and cook for 5 minutes.

8. Remove the lid. Using the back of a large spoon, create 8 wells in the sauce. Gently crack 1 egg into each well. Re-cover the skillet and cook for 6 minutes, or until the egg whites are set. For meal-prep purposes, you may want to slightly undercook the eggs, as they'll continue cooking when reheated.

9. Using a serving spoon, portion 2 eggs and one-fourth of the sauce into each of 4 large single-compartment glass meal-prep containers with tight-fitting lids. Cover and refrigerate.

STORAGE: Keep refrigerated for up to 5 days. Reheat individual portions in the microwave on high power for 1½ to 2 minutes just before eating.

SUBSTITUTION TIP: Swap the kale for any dark leafy green you have on hand, or whatever's in season, such as spinach or Swiss chard.

PER SERVING: Calories: 238; Total Fat: 13g; Saturated Fat: 3g; Protein: 14g; Total Carbohydrates: 15g; Fiber: 5g; Sugar: 8g; Cholesterol: 328mg

Autumn Harvest Squash Bowl, page 136

CHAPTER NINE

Plant-Based Protein Prep

Protein-Packed Five-Bean Salad

SERVES 4

PREP TIME: 15 minutes

DAIRY-FREE

GLUTEN-FREE

NUT-FREE

SOY-FREE

VEGETARIAN

⅔ cup apple cider vinegar

⅓ cup white wine vinegar

⅓ cup sugar

2 tablespoons extra-virgin olive oil

1 teaspoon dried parsley

1 teaspoon granulated garlic

½ teaspoon salt

½ teaspoon freshly ground black pepper

¼ teaspoon celery seed

⅛ teaspoon ground oregano

⅛ teaspoon cayenne pepper

1 red bell pepper, cut into ¼-inch dice

¾ cup thinly sliced red onion

1 (15.5-ounce) can black beans, drained and rinsed

1 (15.5-ounce) can chickpeas, drained and rinsed

1 (15.5-ounce) can cannellini beans, drained and rinsed

2 (15.5-ounce) cans green beans, drained and rinsed

This hearty five-bean salad is full of dietary fiber and plant-based protein, making it a satisfying main course or a delicious side. Dressed with vinegar and plenty of spices, this dish, enjoyed cold or at room temperature, is a flavorful and refreshing addition to any meal-prep plan.

1. In a large bowl, whisk the apple cider vinegar, white wine vinegar, sugar, oil, parsley, garlic, salt, black pepper, celery seed, oregano, and cayenne until combined.

2. Add the red bell pepper, red onion, black beans, chickpeas, cannellini beans, and green beans. Stir well to coat thoroughly.

3. Evenly portion the bean salad into 4 single-compartment glass meal-prep containers with tight-fitting lids. Cover and refrigerate.

STORAGE: Keep refrigerated for up to 5 days. Stir well to redistribute the dressing before enjoying.

INGREDIENT TIP: For an alternate dressing, try Zesty Lemon Vinaigrette (page 83).

PER SERVING: Calories: 475; Total Fat: 11g; Saturated Fat: 1g; Protein: 18g; Total Carbohydrates: 78g; Fiber: 20g; Sugar: 25g; Cholesterol: 0mg

Mediterranean Wheat Berry Salad

SERVES 4

PREP TIME: 20 minutes

NUT-FREE

SOY-FREE

VEGETARIAN

- 2 cups cooked wheat berries (⅓ cup dried)
- 2 medium cucumbers, cut into ½-inch dice
- 1 cup grape tomatoes, halved
- ¼ cup paper-thin red onion slices
- ½ teaspoon sea salt
- ¼ teaspoon freshly ground black pepper
- 1 tablespoon loosely packed chopped fresh basil
- 1 tablespoon loosely packed chopped fresh parsley
- 1 teaspoon loosely packed chopped fresh oregano
- 1 teaspoon minced garlic
- 1 tablespoon red wine vinegar
- 2 teaspoons extra-virgin olive oil
- ⅛ teaspoon red pepper flakes (optional)
- ½ cup crumbled feta cheese

This is our favorite salad to enjoy when the garden and our local farmers' market overflow with fresh tomatoes and cucumbers. Although we like to use wheat berries here for their firm, hearty texture, you can substitute almost any whole grain in this dish, including farro, bulgur, or quinoa, for a gluten-free version.

1. If needed, cook the wheat berries according to the package directions. Set aside.

2. In a large bowl, combine the cucumbers, tomatoes, red onion, salt, and pepper and toss well to combine. Let rest for 10 minutes.

3. Stir the cucumber mixture and add the basil, parsley, oregano, garlic, vinegar, oil, and red pepper flakes (if using). Stir until well combined.

4. Stir in the cooked wheat berries and feta cheese. Let the salad rest for 5 minutes to marinate.

5. Evenly portion the salad into 4 single-compartment glass meal-prep containers with tight-fitting lids. Cover and refrigerate.

STORAGE: Keep refrigerated for up to 5 days. Stir well just before eating to redistribute the marinade.

COOKING TIP: To make the prep for this recipe easier, purchase a pre-cooked grain—frozen cooked quinoa and brown rice are available at many grocery stores.

PER SERVING: Calories: 143; Total Fat: 7g; Saturated Fat: 3g; Protein: 6g; Total Carbohydrates: 18g; Fiber: 3g; Sugar: 4g; Cholesterol: 17mg

Spinach Avocado Chickpea Salad

SERVES 4

PREP TIME: 15 minutes

GLUTEN-FREE
NUT-FREE
SOY-FREE
VEGETARIAN

2 cups Easy Baked
Seasoned Chickpeas
(page 86)

8 tablespoons Zesty Lemon
Vinaigrette (page 83)

2 whole avocados, peeled,
halved, pitted, and diced

1 tablespoon freshly
squeezed lemon juice

1 (8-ounce) package baby
kale and spinach blend

¼ cup freshly grated
Asiago cheese

⅛ teaspoon freshly ground
black pepper

We love the contrasting textures in this salad, with creamy avocado and ultra-crispy Easy Baked Seasoned Chickpeas (page 86). Dressed with fresh, citrusy Zesty Lemon Vinaigrette (page 83) and sprinkled with mild Asiago cheese, this salad is somehow hearty and refreshing all at the same time. We hope it will become a staple in your clean-eating rotation.

1. If needed, prepare the chickpeas and vinaigrette.

2. In a small bowl, toss together the avocados and lemon juice (this will prevent browning). Set aside.

3. Evenly portion the kale and spinach blend into one side of 4 large two-compartment glass meal-prep containers with tight-fitting lids. Top the greens with the avocado, Asiago cheese, and pepper.

4. Evenly portion the chickpeas into the adjacent compartment. Cover and refrigerate.

5. Portion 2 tablespoons of vinaigrette into each of 4 (1½-ounce) stainless-steel salad dressing containers. Cover and refrigerate.

STORAGE: Keep the undressed salad refrigerated for up to 5 days, each paired with a container of Zesty Lemon Vinaigrette. Just before eating, pour the vinaigrette over the salad, secure the lid on the container, and shake well to coat and combine.

COOKING TIP: If you don't have time to prepare the chickpeas, top this salad with any leftover protein you have from earlier preps or use canned chickpeas or tofu.

PER SERVING: Calories: 487; Total Fat: 36g; Saturated Fat: 6g; Protein: 12g; Total Carbohydrates: 33g; Fiber: 12g; Sugar: 6g; Cholesterol: 7mg

Slow Cooker 15-Bean Soup

SERVES 8
PREP TIME: 10 minutes
COOK TIME: 4 to 6 hours

DAIRY-FREE
GLUTEN-FREE
NUT-FREE
SOY-FREE
VEGETARIAN

1 pound dried 15-bean mix, rinsed
10 cups vegetable broth
3 celery stalks, cut into ½-inch dice
3 large carrots, cut into ½-inch dice
1 large onion, cut into ½-inch dice
1 large bay leaf
1 tablespoon whole-grain mustard
1 teaspoon ground turmeric
1 teaspoon kosher salt
½ teaspoon no-salt-added poultry seasoning
½ teaspoon fennel seed
¼ teaspoon freshly ground black pepper
⅛ teaspoon red pepper flakes (optional)

In this recipe, the slow cooker does the work for you and you get a delicious, hearty bean soup practically out of thin air. This low-effort recipe is perfect for meal prep and a great one to keep frozen for a quick lunch or dinner (see Storage tip). Dried beans are an excellent meal-prep pantry staple item: They're extremely affordable, simple to cook, and packed with plant-based nutrition.

1. In a 7-quart slow cooker, combine the beans, vegetable broth, celery, carrots, onion, bay leaf, mustard, turmeric, salt, poultry seasoning, fennel seed, black pepper, and red pepper flakes (if using). Stir well to incorporate.

2. Cover the cooker and cook for 4 to 6 hours on High heat or for 8 to 10 hours on Low heat, until the beans are cooked through and very tender. Remove the bay leaf.

3. Portion 1½ cups of soup each into 4 single-compartment glass meal-prep containers or pint-size Mason jars with tight-fitting lids. You'll have soup left over—portion it into individual single-compartment freezer-safe storage containers with tight-fitting lids. Cover, refrigerate, and freeze.

STORAGE: Keep refrigerated for up to 5 days and keep frozen for up to 2 months. Thaw overnight in the refrigerator. Reheat individual portions in the microwave on high power for 1½ to 2 minutes just before eating.

INGREDIENT TIP: If you can't find a 15-bean mix, any type of dried beans will do.

PER SERVING (1½ CUPS): Calories: 244; Total Fat: 1g; Saturated Fat: 0g; Protein: 13g; Total Carbohydrates: 45g; Fiber: 19g; Sugar: 6g; Cholesterol: 0mg

Vegetarian Hummus Tacos

SERVES 4
PREP TIME: 15 minutes

NUT-FREE

SOY-FREE

VEGETARIAN

2 cups Chipotle Taco
   Hummus (page 85)
1 pint grape tomatoes,
   halved
1 small cucumber, diced
1 bell pepper, any
   color, diced
1 cup canned black beans,
   drained and rinsed
1 cup shredded lettuce
   greens
1 cup full-fat plain
   Greek yogurt
½ cup shredded
   Mexican-style cheese
   (optional)
8 (6-inch) whole-wheat
   tortillas

These super-simple build-your-own tacos are easy to portion for no-fuss assembly on the go. They feature our Chipotle Taco Hummus (page 85), which provides a generous dose of fiber and plant-based protein and we use Greek yogurt as a clean eating–friendly alternative to sour cream. For a low-carb or gluten-free version, serve the tacos in romaine lettuce leaves instead of tortillas.

1. If needed, make the hummus.

2. In a large bowl, toss together the tomatoes, cucumber, bell pepper, and black beans. Set aside.

3. Evenly portion the shredded greens into the largest wells of 3 three-compartment glass meal-prep containers with tight-fitting lids. Top the greens with the vegetable mixture.

4. Portion ½ cup of hummus into one of the smaller compartments of each container.

5. Portion ¼ cup of yogurt into the remaining small compartments of each container. Top each portion of yogurt with 2 tablespoons of shredded cheese (if using). Cover and refrigerate.

6. Wrap 4 sets of 2 tortillas each in parchment paper followed by plastic wrap.

STORAGE: Keep refrigerated for up to 5 days, each container paired with a set of tortillas. When ready to eat, top the tortillas with hummus, followed by the greens and vegetables, yogurt, and cheese (if using). Fold into tacos and enjoy.

SUBSTITUTION TIP: If you don't have time to make the hummus, use store-bought hummus—just check the ingredients to ensure it doesn't contain any unwanted additives or preservatives.

PER SERVING: Calories: 548; Total Fat: 16g; Saturated Fat: 6g; Protein: 26g; Total Carbohydrates: 81g; Fiber: 18g; Sugar: 14g; Cholesterol: 22mg

Veggie Fried Rice Bowl

SERVES 4
PREP TIME: 20 minutes
COOK TIME: 15 minutes

DAIRY-FREE

GLUTEN-FREE

NUT-FREE

SOY-FREE

2 cups cooked brown rice, cooled completely (about ⅔ cup dried)

¼ cup vegetable broth

¼ cup coconut aminos

1 teaspoon minced garlic

1 teaspoon freshly squeezed lime juice

1 tablespoon grated peeled fresh ginger, divided

½ teaspoon sugar

2 tablespoons sesame oil, divided

4 large eggs, beaten

½ cup chopped scallions, white and green parts separated

2 cups shredded green cabbage

1 cup shredded red cabbage

2 cups shredded carrots

This fried rice bowl is our clean-eating tribute to takeout, and we have to say, it more than satisfies the craving. Sesame oil is key to achieving the toasted nutty flavor here and you can find it at almost any grocery store. If you don't have coconut aminos, use soy sauce (just be aware that the dish will no longer be soy-free or gluten-free). We enjoy this dish as is, but it's also great for using up leftover pork, chicken, or shrimp.

1. If needed, cook the brown rice according to the package instructions. Let cool completely.

2. In a large bowl, whisk the vegetable broth, coconut aminos, garlic, lime juice, 1 teaspoon of ginger, and sugar until the sugar is dissolved. Set aside.

3. Heat a large skillet or wok over medium-high heat. Add 1 tablespoon of oil and the eggs and begin stirring immediately to prevent the oil from burning. Scramble the eggs for about 1 minute into small pieces until just cooked. Remove the eggs from the pan and set aside.

4. Adjust the heat to high. Place the scallion whites in the center of the skillet and cook for 1 minute, until softened, stirring constantly. Push the scallions to the outer edges of the skillet.

5. Place the green cabbage in the center of pan and cook for 1 minute, until slightly tender, stirring constantly. Push the cabbage to the outer edges of the pan with the scallions.

6. Repeat the process used in steps 4 and 5 for the remaining vegetables, in the following order: red cabbage, carrots, and, finally, the remaining 2 teaspoons of ginger.

7. Once the ginger is fragrant, add the remaining 1 tablespoon of oil and the cooked rice. Cook, stirring constantly, for 1 minute until the fried rice starts to smell toasted.

8. Still in all the vegetables from the edges of the skillet and mix well to incorporate.

9. Pour in the sauce from step 2 and stir until fully incorporated. Cook for about 2 minutes until reduced by roughly half. Remove the pan from the heat and stir in the scrambled eggs and scallion greens.

10. Evenly portion the fried rice into 4 single-compartment glass meal-prep containers with tight-fitting lids. Cover and refrigerate.

STORAGE: Keep refrigerated for up to 5 days. Reheat individual portions in the microwave on high power for 1½ to 2 minutes just before eating. If the rice is dried out, add water, 1 tablespoon at a time, for moisture.

INGREDIENT TIP: To reduce prep time, look for shredded cabbage and shredded carrots in the grocery store produce section (or use shredded coleslaw mix). Pre-cooked frozen brown rice from the grocery store is also a huge time-saver here.

PER SERVING: Calories: 320; Total Fat: 13g; Saturated Fat: 3g; Protein: 10g; Total Carbohydrates: 39g; Fiber: 5g; Sugar: 9g; Cholesterol: 187mg

Baked Broccoli-Cheddar Bites

SERVES 4
PREP TIME: 15 minutes
COOK TIME: 30 minutes

NUT-FREE

SOY-FREE

2 teaspoons extra-virgin
   olive oil, divided
3 to 4 quarts water
6 cups broccoli florets
4 cups packed
   chopped kale
¾ cup diced yellow onion
2 garlic cloves, peeled
½ cup loosely packed
   chopped fresh parsley
3 large eggs
1 cup shredded sharp
   Cheddar cheese
½ cup grated Parmesan
¾ cup bread crumbs
½ teaspoon freshly ground
   black pepper
¼ teaspoon salt
8 tablespoons Creamy
   Ranch Dressing (page 84)

Move over, tater-tots! These cheesy broccoli bites are the perfect meal prep–friendly finger food. Baked rather than fried, these bite-size morsels are crispy and delicious but healthy—they're packed with veggies, after all. These are great to make ahead and keep frozen for up to 2 months. We like to dip them in Creamy Ranch Dressing (page 84), but you can also try Chipotle Taco Hummus (page 85) for a change of pace.

1. Preheat the oven to 400°F. Line 2 baking sheets with foil and brush each with 1 teaspoon of oil. Set aside.

2. In a large stockpot over high heat, bring the water to a boil. Add the broccoli florets and return the water to a boil. Cook for 2 minutes, until the florets are bright green.

3. Add the kale to the pot, return the water to a boil, and cook for 1 to 2 minutes, just until the kale is bright green. Turn off the heat, quickly drain the hot water and run the broccoli and kale under cold water to stop the cooking. Set aside.

4. In the bowl of a food processor, combine the onion, garlic, and parsley. Pulse until finely minced. Add the cooked broccoli and kale and pulse in 15-second intervals until broken down into small pieces. Add the eggs, Cheddar and Parmesan cheeses, bread crumbs, pepper, and salt. Continue pulsing until the mixture is fully incorporated and uniform in texture.

5. Using clean hands, form the mixture into 48 balls, about 1½ inches in diameter, and place them on the prepared baking sheets evenly spaced. Press down slightly on the balls to form small patties, about ½ inch thick and 2 inches in diameter.

6. Bake the broccoli bites for 10 minutes. Using a spatula, flip the bites and bake for 10 more minutes, or until golden brown on both sides.

7. While the broccoli bites cook, make the ranch dressing, if necessary. Portion 2 tablespoons of dressing into each of 4 (1½-ounce) stainless-steel salad dressing containers. Cover the containers.

8. Evenly portion the broccoli bites (about 12 bites each) into 4 single-compartment glass meal-prep containers with tight-fitting lids. Cover and refrigerate with the dressing containers.

STORAGE: Keep refrigerated for up to 5 days, each paired with a container of Creamy Ranch Dressing. Reheat individual portions in the microwave on high power for 1½ to 2 minutes just before eating.

INGREDIENT TIP: If you don't have fresh broccoli on hand, frozen, thawed broccoli works perfectly in this recipe.

PER SERVING (12 BITES): Calories: 412; Total Fat: 21g; Saturated Fat: 10g; Protein: 24g; Total Carbohydrates: 31g; Fiber: 6g; Sugar: 6g; Cholesterol: 167mg

Greens & Beans–Stuffed Mushrooms

SERVES 4
PREP TIME: 15 minutes
COOK TIME: 20 minutes

GLUTEN-FREE

NUT-FREE

SOY-FREE

VEGETARIAN

Nonstick cooking spray
4 tablespoons olive
   oil, divided
4 portabella mushroom
   caps, 4 to 5 inches wide
½ teaspoon salt
½ teaspoon freshly ground
   black pepper
2 tablespoons
   minced garlic
8 cups baby kale
1 cup vegetable broth
2 (15.5-ounce) cans white
   cannellini beans, drained
   and rinsed
¼ cup freshly squeezed
   lemon juice
½ cup shredded mozzarella

If you're a mushroom lover, these luxurious stuffed mushrooms, filled with lemon-garlic greens and beans, are the perfect dinner for you. Mushrooms offer an excellent source of many important nutrients and their rich, earthy umami flavor and hearty texture give them an almost meat-like quality. Though 100 percent vegetarian, this dish easily stands on its own as a dinner entrée.

1. Preheat the oven to 375°F. Line a baking sheet with foil, coat it with cooking spray, and set aside.

2. Lightly drizzle 1 tablespoon of oil over the mushroom caps. Flip and drizzle 1 tablespoon of oil on the gill side. Season with salt and pepper and transfer to the baking prepared sheet, gill-side up.

3. Roast for 10 minutes.

4. While the mushrooms cook, in a cast-iron skillet over medium heat, heat the remaining 2 tablespoons of oil. Add the garlic and cook for 1 minute. Add 1 handful of kale and let it cook down. Once it begins to wilt, add a bit of the vegetable broth and let it continue to cook down. Continue alternating handfuls of kale with a bit of vegetable broth, letting the kale cook down between additions until all of it is added.

5. Stir in the beans and lemon juice. Cook for 2 minutes, stirring frequently, until most of the liquid is evaporated. Remove from the heat.

6. Remove the roasted mushrooms from the oven. Evenly portion the kale and beans into the mushroom caps.

7. Sprinkle each mushroom cap with 2 tablespoons of mozzarella. Return the mushrooms to the oven for 3 minutes, or until the cheese has melted and is lightly golden brown.

8. Portion 1 stuffed mushroom into each of 4 single-compartment glass meal-prep containers with tight-fitting lids. Cover and refrigerate.

STORAGE: Keep refrigerated for up to 5 days. Reheat individual portions in the microwave on high power for 1½ to 2 minutes just before eating.

INGREDIENT TIP: For an even heartier stuffed mushroom, add 1 pound of ground pork, chicken, or turkey during step 4, ensuring that the meat cooks through completely.

PER SERVING: Calories: 386; Total Fat: 20g; Saturated Fat: 4g; Protein: 17g; Total Carbohydrates: 38g; Fiber: 12g; Sugar: 5g; Cholesterol: 13mg

Autumn Harvest Squash Bowl

SERVES 4
PREP TIME: 15 minutes
COOK TIME: 30 minutes

DAIRY-FREE
GLUTEN-FREE
NUT-FREE
SOY-FREE
VEGETARIAN

2 cups cooked quinoa
  (⅔ cup dried)
2 small delicata squash,
  halved, seeded, and
  cut into ½-inch-thick
  half-moons
1 (15.5-ounce) can chick-
  peas, drained and rinsed
2 teaspoons extra-virgin
  olive oil
½ teaspoon salt
½ teaspoon freshly ground
  black pepper
¼ teaspoon ground
  cinnamon
⅛ teaspoon paprika
4 thyme sprigs
¼ cup dried cranberries
¼ cup pumpkin seeds
1 (8-ounce) package
  chopped kale
¼ cup maple syrup

Delicata squash is one of only a few winter squash varieties with an edible rind, making it one of our favorites for meal prep. As a clean-eating bonus, the skin of the squash has plenty of vitamins, fiber, and other health benefits. We like to make this dish in the fall, when delicata squash is at peak season. With cinnamon, sweet dried cranberries, and crunchy pumpkin seeds, this dish is practically autumn in a bowl.

1. If needed, cook the quinoa according to the package directions.

2. Preheat the oven to 350°F. Line a large baking sheet with foil and set aside.

3. In a large bowl, combine the squash, chickpeas, oil, salt, pepper, cinnamon, paprika, and thyme sprigs. Toss to incorporate. Spread the mixture into an even layer on the prepared baking sheet.

4. Roast for 30 minutes. Remove the baking sheet from the oven and sprinkle the mixture with the cranberries and pumpkin seeds. Return to the oven and bake for 5 minutes more.

5. While the squash roasts, evenly portion the kale into 4 large single-compartment glass meal-prep containers with tight-fitting lids.

6. Evenly divide the cooked quinoa, the warm ingredients from the baking pan, and the maple syrup among the containers, on top of the kale (the warmth of the quinoa will help steam the kale in the containers). Cover and refrigerate.

STORAGE: Keep refrigerated for up to 5 days and enjoy cold or warm. Reheat individual portions in the microwave at high power for 1½ to 2 minutes just before eating.

COOKING TIP: To make this prep easier, look for cooked quinoa or brown rice, often available in grocery store freezer sections.

PER SERVING: Calories: 457; Total Fat: 11g; Saturated Fat: 2g; Protein: 14g; Total Carbohydrates: 83g; Fiber: 17g; Sugar: 25g; Cholesterol: 0mg

Summer Vegetable Ratatouille Bake

SERVES 8
PREP TIME: 15 minutes
COOK TIME: 1 hour

DAIRY-FREE
GLUTEN-FREE
NUT-FREE
SOY-FREE
VEGETARIAN

1 teaspoon extra-virgin
olive oil plus 1 tablespoon
1 (12-ounce) eggplant cut
into ¼-inch rounds
2 teaspoons salt, divided
1 (28-ounce) can diced
tomatoes and juices
2 tablespoons balsamic
vinegar
2 tablespoons
minced garlic
½ cup thinly sliced scallions,
white and green parts
¼ cup loosely packed fresh
basil, chopped
½ teaspoon herbes de
Provence
¼ teaspoon freshly ground
black pepper
⅛ teaspoon red pepper
flakes (optional)
1 or 2 zucchini (12 ounces),
cut into ¼-inch rounds
1 or 2 yellow squash
(12 ounces), cut into
¼-inch rounds

This deliciously elegant baked ratatouille is an easy one-pan dish, filled with nutritious, hearty eggplant, zucchini, and yellow squash. This dish is at its best during late summertime, when eggplants and summer squash are at peak season. This dish stands on its own as a meal, but for added protein, pair it with baked chicken or fish.

1. Preheat the oven to 375°F. Brush a 9-by-13-inch glass baking dish with 1 teaspoon of oil and set aside.

2. Lay out the eggplant slices on a work surface. Sprinkle with 1 teaspoon of salt and let sit for at least 10 minutes while preparing the rest of the dish.

3. In a large bowl, stir together the tomatoes and their juices, vinegar, garlic, scallions, basil, remaining 1 teaspoon of salt, herbes de Provence, black pepper, and red pepper flakes (if using). Transfer half the mixture to the prepared baking dish, spreading it in an even layer.

4. Blot the salted eggplant with a clean towel to wick away excess moisture. Stack the eggplant, zucchini, and yellow squash in 3 or 4 rows, alternating in a pattern (e.g. eggplant, zucchini, yellow squash, eggplant, and so on) to fill the baking dish.

5. Pour the remaining tomato mixture over the vegetables to cover them. Drizzle the ratatouille with the remaining 1 tablespoon of oil.

6. Cover the baking dish with foil and bake for 40 minutes. Remove the foil and bake for 20 minutes more.

7. Portion half the ratatouille into 4 single-compartment glass meal-prep containers with tight-fitting lids. Cover and refrigerate. Portion the remaining half into 4 airtight freezer-safe containers with lids. Cover and freeze.

STORAGE: Keep refrigerated for up to 5 days and frozen for up to 2 months. Thaw in the refrigerator overnight. Reheat individual portions in the microwave on high power for 1½ to 2 minutes just before eating.

INGREDIENT TIP: If you don't have eggplant available, use more zucchini or yellow squash in its place.

PER SERVING: Calories: 79; Total Fat: 3g; Saturated Fat: 1g; Protein: 2g; Total Carbohydrates: 11g; Fiber: 4g; Sugar: 6g; Cholesterol: 0mg

Kale & Bean–Stuffed Sweet Potatoes

SERVES 4
PREP TIME: 15 minutes
COOK TIME: 30 minutes

DAIRY-FREE
GLUTEN-FREE
NUT-FREE
SOY-FREE
VEGETARIAN

2 tablespoons Homemade
   Taco Seasoning (page 82)
4 sweet potatoes, washed,
   skins on
1 tablespoon extra-virgin
   olive oil
1 cup diced onion
2 cups chopped kale
1 (15-ounce) can black
   beans, drained
   and rinsed
1 avocado, peeled, halved,
   pitted, and diced
1 cup cherry tomatoes,
   diced
1 tablespoon chopped fresh
   cilantro
1 tablespoon freshly
   squeezed lemon juice

Sweet potatoes make a great foundation for a fill-ing plant-based meal and this dish was inspired by our love of tacos. In this recipe, the natural delicate sugars in the sweet potatoes perfectly comple-ment the spices in our Homemade Taco Seasoning (page 82), and black beans and kale make this a hearty entrée. Topped with fresh avocado and tomato, this dish is a fun new way to enjoy an old favorite.

1. Preheat the oven to 450°F.

2. If needed, prepare the taco seasoning.

3. Pierce each sweet potato with a fork multiple times to allow steam to escape and wrap individu-ally in foil. Place the wrapped sweet potatoes on a large baking sheet.

4. Bake for 30 minutes, until the potatoes are easily pierced with a fork.

5. Meanwhile, in a medium skillet or sauté pan over medium heat, heat the oil. Add the onion and cook for 2 minutes, or until translucent.

6. One handful at a time, add the kale, letting each handful wilt before adding the next. Once all the kale is wilted and cooked down, stir in the black beans and taco seasoning. Cook for 2 minutes, stirring frequently. Remove from the heat.

7. Remove the sweet potatoes from the oven and set aside to cool.

8. In a small bowl, toss to combine the avocado, tomatoes, cilantro, and lemon juice.

9. Once the sweet potatoes are cool enough to handle, remove the foil. Carefully slit open the sweet potatoes lengthwise to release the steam. Evenly portion the kale and bean mixture into the center of the sweet potatoes.

10. Place each stuffed sweet potato in one section of 4 large two-compartment glass meal-prep containers with tight-fitting lids. Fill the adjacent compartment with the avocado and tomato mixture. Cover and refrigerate.

STORAGE: Keep refrigerated for up to 5 days. Reheat the stuffed sweet potatoes in the microwave on high power for 1½ to 2 minutes just before eating. Do not reheat the avocado and tomato mixture. Top the sweet potatoes with the avocado-tomato mixture and enjoy.

COOKING TIP: To reduce cooking time, cook the sweet potatoes in the microwave. Pierce them several times with a fork to allow steam to escape, wrap them in damp paper towels, and microwave on high power for about 4 minutes per potato, or 15 minutes for 4, until easily pierced with a fork.

PER SERVING: Calories: 411; Total Fat: 10g; Saturated Fat: 1g; Protein: 12g; Total Carbohydrates: 73g; Fiber: 19g; Sugar: 12g; Cholesterol: 0mg

Lemon-Herb Chicken Meatballs, page 148

CHAPTER TEN

Animal-Based Protein Prep

Grilled Tandoori Chicken Legs

SERVES 4

PREP TIME: 15 minutes, plus 2 hours to marinate

COOK TIME: 30 minutes

GLUTEN-FREE

NUT-FREE

SOY-FREE

2 pounds chicken legs (8 drumsticks)

1½ tablespoons paprika

1 tablespoon ground cumin

2 teaspoons garlic powder

2 teaspoons onion powder

2 teaspoons ground ginger

2 teaspoons kosher salt

1½ teaspoons ground coriander

1 teaspoon ground turmeric

½ teaspoon ground cinnamon

½ teaspoon freshly ground black pepper

¼ teaspoon cayenne pepper

⅛ teaspoon ground cloves

⅛ teaspoon ground nutmeg

1 cup full-fat plain Greek yogurt

¼ cup freshly squeezed lemon juice

Tandoori chicken—popular in some regional Indian cuisines—refers to yogurt-marinated spiced chicken cooked in a tandoor, a metal or clay oven that reaches super-high temperatures. In our tandoori-inspired dish, the chicken is cooked instead on a grill. Full-fat Greek yogurt provides important dietary fats and protein and it also helps to break down the chicken, resulting in tender, juicy drumsticks. Try this chicken with the Caprese Salad Grain Bowl (page 49).

1. Place the drumsticks in an airtight bag or container for marinating—we recommend a gallon-size zip-top bag. Set aside.

2. In a large bowl, combine the paprika, cumin, garlic powder, onion powder, ginger, salt, coriander, turmeric, cinnamon, black pepper, cayenne, cloves, and nutmeg. Add the yogurt and lemon juice and stir until well incorporated. Pour the yogurt mixture over the drumsticks to coat them thoroughly. Seal the container and refrigerate the drumsticks to marinate for at least 2 hours, ideally overnight.

3. Preheat a grill to medium-high heat.

4. Remove the drumsticks from the marinade and place them on the hot grill. Discard any remaining marinade. Grill for 5 to 7 minutes per side, rotating 4 or 5 times (total cooking time will be about 30 minutes, depending on the size of the drumsticks). The chicken is done once it reaches an internal temperature of 165°F.

5. Portion 2 drumsticks into one half of 4 large two-compartment glass meal-prep containers with tight-fitting lids. Fill the remaining compartment with a side of your choice. Cover and refrigerate.

STORAGE: Keep refrigerated for up to 5 days. Reheat individual portions of chicken in the microwave on high power for 1½ to 2 minutes just before eating.

COOKING TIP: To make additional tandoori sauce for dipping, reserve ½ cup of yogurt marinade from step 2 for serving before adding the chicken. To bake the drumsticks indoors, roast at 400°F for 40 to 50 minutes, or until the chicken reaches an internal temperature of 165°F.

PER SERVING: Calories: 514; Total Fat: 28g; Saturated Fat: 8g; Protein: 55g; Total Carbohydrates: 9g; Fiber: 2g; Sugar: 3g; Cholesterol: 254mg

Super-Simple Baked Chicken

SERVES 4
PREP TIME: 5 minutes
COOK TIME: 15 minutes

DAIRY-FREE

GLUTEN-FREE

NUT-FREE

SOY-FREE

1½ teaspoons extra-virgin
    olive oil, divided
1 pound chicken breast, cut
    into 1-inch strips
½ teaspoon salt
½ teaspoon freshly
    squeezed lemon juice
⅛ teaspoon freshly ground
    black pepper

This one-pan baked chicken is the simplest and most versatile of all our meal-prep recipes. By varying the spices, herbs, and other seasonings, you can easily customize this chicken to fit almost any meal. (Try paprika, cumin, chili powder, or rosemary.) Once cooked, you can also dice or shred the chicken to use in salads, tacos, sand-wiches, and more.

1. Preheat the oven to 400°F. Line a baking sheet with foil and brush it with 1 teaspoon of oil. Set aside.

2. In a large bowl, combine the remaining ½ teaspoon of oil, chicken, salt, lemon juice, and pepper. Toss well to coat thoroughly. Transfer the seasoned chicken to the prepared baking sheet and spread it into a single layer.

3. Bake for 15 minutes, or until the chicken reaches an internal temperature of 165°F.

4. Evenly portion the chicken into one well of 4 large two- or three-compartment glass meal-prep containers with tight-fitting lids. Fill the remaining compartments with sides and salads of your choice, such as vegetables and quinoa or Autumn Harvest Squash Bowl (page 136). Cover and refrigerate.

STORAGE: Keep refrigerated for up to 5 days. Reheat individual portions of chicken in the microwave for 1½ to 2 minutes just before eating.

COOKING TIP: To stretch this dish further, add sliced fresh vegetables to the baking sheet to roast alongside the chicken. We like to add bell pepper and carrots.

PER SERVING: Calories: 145; Total Fat: 5g; Saturated Fat: 1g; Protein: 25g; Total Carbohydrates: 0g; Fiber: 0g; Sugar: 0g; Cholesterol: 80mg

Braised Chicken Marsala

SERVES 4
PREP TIME: 10 minutes
COOK TIME: 50 minutes

GLUTEN-FREE

NUT-FREE

SOY-FREE

1½ pounds boneless, skinless chicken thighs

1 pound cremini mushrooms, stemmed, cut into ¼-inch slices

2 teaspoons minced garlic

1 tablespoon freshly squeezed lemon juice

1 teaspoon dried parsley

½ teaspoon salt

¼ teaspoon freshly ground black pepper

¾ cup Marsala wine

3 tablespoons butter

Marsala is a fortified Italian wine commonly used in cooking—for those of us who grew up in Italian households, its distinctive flavor evokes a classic comfort-food feeling. Our lightened-up version of this chicken dish, cooked in a rich broth, results in tender, flavorful meat and still captures all the full-bodied flavor of Marsala. Try pairing this chicken with Spiralized Zucchini Panzanella Salad (page 29).

1. Preheat the oven to 325°F.

2. Arrange the chicken thighs in a single layer in an oven-safe baking dish. Top with the mushrooms and garlic and drizzle with lemon juice. Sprinkle with parsley, salt, and pepper.

3. Pour the Marsala wine over the entire mixture. Place dabs of the butter across the chicken and mushrooms, evenly spaced.

4. Place the dish in the oven and bake for 50 minutes, or until the chicken reaches an internal temperature of 165°F.

5. Evenly portion the chicken thighs and mushroom sauce into one half of 4 large two-compartment glass meal-prep containers with tight-fitting lids. Fill the remaining compartment with a side or salad of your choice. Cover and refrigerate.

STORAGE: Keep refrigerated for up to 5 days. Reheat individual portions of chicken Marsala in the microwave on high power for 1½ to 2 minutes just before eating.

COOKING TIP: If you want to get in an extra serving of veggies, add 2 cups of cauliflower or broccoli florets to the baking dish during step 2.

PER SERVING: Calories: 373; Total Fat: 19g; Saturated Fat: 6g; Protein: 31g; Total Carbohydrates: 12g; Fiber: 1g; Sugar: 6g; Cholesterol: 160mg

Lemon-Herb Chicken Meatballs

SERVES 4
PREP TIME: 20 minutes
COOK TIME: 20 minutes

NUT-FREE

SOY-FREE

¼ cup whole-wheat
  bread crumbs
¼ cup milk
¼ cup loosely packed fresh
  parsley, finely chopped
3 tablespoons finely minced
  yellow onion
2 tablespoons finely
  minced celery
2 tablespoons freshly
  squeezed lemon juice
1 tablespoon coconut
  aminos
1 tablespoon finely
  minced garlic
1½ teaspoons minced
  peeled fresh ginger
¼ teaspoon salt
¼ teaspoon freshly ground
  black pepper
1 large egg, beaten
1 pound ground chicken
1 tablespoon extra-virgin
  olive oil

These flavorful chicken meatballs are a delicious and filling snack or entrée on their own, but they also pair perfectly with any vegetable side dish. We love to prep double batches of these meatballs and freeze them to enjoy later over zucchini noodles (topped with red sauce) or use them as a staple protein in salads, wraps, and more. Try pairing them with Baked Broccoli-Cheddar Bites (page 132).

1. Preheat the oven to 400°F.

2. In a small bowl, stir together the bread crumbs and milk. Set aside to soak.

3. Meanwhile, in a large bowl, combine the parsley, onion, celery, lemon juice, coconut aminos, garlic, ginger, salt, and pepper. Mix well to incorporate.

4. Stir in the soaked bread crumbs and beaten egg and mix until well incorporated. Add the ground chicken and, using clean hands, gently fold the ingredients together until they form a cohesive mixture. Be careful not to overmix. Roll the mixture into about 16 (1½-inch) meatballs and set aside on a plate.

5. In a large oven-safe skillet or Dutch oven over medium-high heat, heat the oil. Carefully add the meatballs and brown on one side for 3 to 5 minutes. Flip and brown the other side for 3 to 5 minutes more.

6. Place the skillet in the oven and bake the meatballs for 10 minutes, or until they reach an internal temperature of 165°F.

7. Evenly divide the meatballs among one half of 4 large two-compartment glass meal-prep containers with tight-fitting lids. Fill the remaining compartment with a side or salad of your choice. Cover and refrigerate.

STORAGE: Keep refrigerated for up to 5 days, or freeze for up to 2 months in airtight freezer-safe containers. Thaw in the refrigerator overnight. Reheat individual portions in the microwave on high power for 1½ to 2 minutes just before eating.

INGREDIENT TIP: To make savory beef meatballs, swap the ground chicken for ground beef, the parsley for cilantro, and the lemon juice for lime juice.

PER SERVING (4 MEATBALLS): Calories: 257; Total Fat: 15g; Saturated Fat: 4g; Protein: 23g; Total Carbohydrates: 9g; Fiber: 1g; Sugar: 3g; Cholesterol: 146mg

Togarashi Grilled Turkey Steaks

SERVES 4
PREP TIME: 10 minutes, plus 1 hour to marinate
COOK TIME: 10 minutes

DAIRY-FREE
GLUTEN-FREE
NUT-FREE
SOY-FREE

1 pound turkey breast, cut into 4 (½-inch-thick) steaks
2 tablespoons coconut aminos
1 tablespoon freshly squeezed lime juice
1 tablespoon light brown sugar
1 tablespoon water
½ teaspoon sesame oil
1 tablespoon togarashi spice

Togarashi is a Japanese seven-spice seasoning blend with a spicy, citrusy flavor profile. This spice lends a delicious, flavorful coating to these lean turkey steaks. We raise our own turkeys but highly recommend checking out your local butcher to find delicious, locally raised turkey as a high-quality meat option. If you can't find togarashi at your grocery store or online, Cajun seasoning makes a great substitute. Try pairing this turkey with Protein-Packed Five-Bean Salad (page 124).

1. Place the turkey breast in an airtight bag or container for marinating—we recommend a gallon-size zip-top bag. Set aside.

2. In a large bowl, whisk the coconut aminos, lime juice, brown sugar, water, and oil to incorporate. Pour the marinade over the turkey to thoroughly coat it. Seal the bag and refrigerate to marinate for at least 1 hour, ideally overnight.

3. Preheat a grill to medium-high heat.

4. Remove the turkey from the marinade and discard any remaining marinade. Evenly season both sides of each turkey steak with togarashi spice and place the turkey on the hot grill. Cook the turkey steaks for 2 to 3 minutes per side, or until the turkey reaches an internal temperature of 155°F. Remove the turkey breasts from the grill and wrap them tightly in foil. Let rest for 10 minutes, or until the turkey reaches an internal temperature of 165°F.

5. Place 1 turkey steak into one side of 4 large two-compartment glass meal-prep containers with tight-fitting ides. Fill the remaining compartment with a side or salad of your choice. Cover and refrigerate.

STORAGE: Keep refrigerated for up to 5 days. Reheat individual portions in the microwave on high power for 1½ to 2 minutes just before eating.

INGREDIENT TIP: The turkey steaks will continue cooking once removed from the heat—we take them off the grill at 155°F to prevent them from overcooking and becoming tough. If you can't find turkey breast, use chicken breast instead.

PER SERVING: Calories: 151; Total Fat: 2g; Saturated Fat: <1g; Protein: 27g; Total Carbohydrates: 4g; Fiber: 0g; Sugar: 4g; Cholesterol: 64mg

Apple Barbecue Pulled Pork

SERVES 4
PREP TIME: 20 minutes
COOK TIME: 6 to 8 hours

DAIRY-FREE
NUT-FREE
SOY-FREE

1 cup unsweetened
applesauce
½ cup yellow mustard
¼ cup honey
¼ cup apple cider vinegar
1 tablespoon freshly
squeezed lemon juice
2 teaspoons Worcester-
shire sauce
1 teaspoon salt, divided
½ teaspoon freshly ground
black pepper, divided
¼ teaspoon red pepper
flakes (optional)
1½ pounds boneless
pork butt
1 tablespoon avocado oil

This delicious sweet-and-savory slow-cooker pulled pork will leave your house smelling incredible on meal-prep day. Use pulled pork on sandwiches, in wraps, or to top salads, though we often also enjoy this protein staple on its own. We recommend pairing it with the Jerk-Seasoned Waldorf Salad (page 50).

1. In a large bowl, whisk the apple sauce, mustard, honey, vinegar, lemon juice, Worcestershire sauce, ½ teaspoon of salt, ¼ teaspoon of black pepper, and red pepper flakes (if using). Set aside.

2. Sprinkle the remaining ½ teaspoon of salt and remaining ¼ teaspoon of pepper onto both sides of the pork butt.

3. In a large skillet over medium-high heat, heat the oil until very hot. Add the pork butt to the hot skillet and sear for 1 minute. Flip and sear the other side for 1 minute. Transfer the seared pork to a 7-quart slow cooker and top with the applesauce mixture.

4. Cover the cooker and cook on Low heat for 6 to 8 hours, or until the meat is cooked through and easily falls apart when prodded with a fork. Let cool until you can handle it, then shred the meat with 2 forks.

5. Evenly divide the pulled pork among 4 large two-compartment glass meal-prep containers with tight-fitting lids. Fill the remaining compartment with a side or salad of your choice. Cover and refrigerate.

STORAGE: Keep refrigerated for up to 5 days. Reheat individual portions in the microwave on high power for 1½ to 2 minutes just before eating.

INGREDIENT TIP: If you don't eat pork, substitute boneless, skinless chicken thighs.

PER SERVING: Calories: 460; Total Fat: 26g; Saturated Fat: 8g; Protein: 31g; Total Carbohydrates: 27g; Fiber: 2g; Sugar: 24g; Cholesterol: 105mg

Baked Herbed Lamb Meatloaf

SERVES 4
PREP TIME: 15 minutes
COOK TIME: 1 hour

NUT-FREE

SOY-FREE

1 tablespoon extra-virgin olive oil

¼ cup whole-wheat bread crumbs

¼ cup milk

2 pounds ground lamb

2 large eggs, beaten

½ cup minced red onion

½ cup minced Kalamata olives

½ cup chopped fresh parsley

1 teaspoon chopped fresh mint

1 teaspoon chopped fresh oregano

½ teaspoon chopped fresh thyme

½ teaspoon salt

This baked meatloaf is perfect for meal prep because it can be enjoyed as a hot entrée or cooled and thinly cut into gyro-style meat for sandwiches, wraps, salads, and more. The fresh herbs in this preparation give this meatloaf bold, complex flavors. You can find nutritious lean ground lamb at most local farm stores. Pair this meatloaf with a refreshing Crunchy Kale Salad (page 71).

1. Preheat the oven to 350°F. Coat a loaf pan or baking dish with olive oil and set aside.

2. In a small bowl, stir together the bread crumbs and milk. Set aside to soak.

3. Meanwhile, in a large bowl, combine the ground lamb, eggs, red onion, olives, parsley, mint, oregano, thyme, and salt. Using clean hands, fold together the ingredients until a cohesive mixture forms.

4. Add the soaked bread crumbs and continue mixing to incorporate. Press the mixture evenly into the prepared loaf pan.

5. Bake the meatloaf for 50 minutes to 1 hour, or until it reaches an internal temperature of 165°F. Let rest for at least 30 minutes before cutting into 8 slices.

6. Portion 2 slices of meatloaf into one side of 4 large two-compartment glass meal-prep containers with tight-fitting lids. Fill the remaining compartment with a side or salad of your choice. Cover and refrigerate.

STORAGE: Keep refrigerated for up to 5 days. Reheat individual portions in the microwave on high power for 1½ to 2 minutes just before eating.

INGREDIENT TIP: If you can't find or don't enjoy ground lamb, use lean ground beef instead.

PER SERVING: Calories: 710; Total Fat: 56g; Saturated Fat: 24g; Protein: 44g; Total Carbohydrates: 9g; Fiber: 2g; Sugar: 3g; Cholesterol: 249mg

Pot Roast Beef Stroganoff

SERVES 4
PREP TIME: 20 minutes
COOK TIME: 6 to 8 hours

NUT-FREE
SOY-FREE

1 pound cremini mushrooms, stemmed, cut into ¼-inch-thick slices
2 white onions, cut into ¼-inch slices
1½ cups beef broth
2 tablespoons Worcestershire sauce
2 tablespoons minced garlic
2 bay leaves
1 teaspoon dried thyme
1 teaspoon dried rosemary
1 teaspoon salt, divided
¼ teaspoon freshly ground black pepper, divided
1 tablespoon avocado oil
2 pounds chuck roast
1 cup full-fat plain Greek yogurt

This is a clean-eating version of one of our favorite meals—classic beef stroganoff. By using full-fat Greek yogurt in this recipe, we were able to create a delicious, savory cream sauce without using the typical butter and sour cream—offering a higher amount of protein and far less saturated fat. This rich dish pairs nicely with a light, fresh Crunchy Kale Salad (page 71).

1. In a 7-quart slow cooker, combine the mushrooms, onions, beef broth, Worcestershire sauce, garlic, bay leaves, thyme, rosemary, and ½ teaspoon of salt. Set aside.

2. Sprinkle the remaining ½ teaspoon of salt and the pepper onto both sides of the chuck roast.

3. In a large skillet over medium-high heat, heat the oil until very hot. Add the chuck roast to the hot skillet and sear for 1 minute. Flip and sear the other side for 1 minute. Transfer the seared chuck roast to the slow cooker, placing it on top of the mushrooms.

4. Cover the cooker and cook on Low heat for 6 to 8 hours, or until the meat is cooked through and easily falls apart when prodded with a fork. Let cool until you can handle it, then shred the meat with 2 forks.

5. Add the yogurt to the slow cooker and stir to incorporate until the mixture is smooth and creamy. Remove the bay leaves.

6. Evenly portion the stroganoff into one half of 4 large two-compartment glass meal-prep containers with tight-fitting lids. Fill the remaining compartment with a side or salad of your choice. Cover and refrigerate.

STORAGE: Keep refrigerated for up to 5 days. Reheat individual portions in the microwave on high power for 1½ to 2 minutes just before eating.

PER SERVING: Calories: 692; Total Fat: 46g; Saturated Fat: 18g; Protein: 54g; Total Carbohydrates: 15g; Fiber: 2g; Sugar: 7g; Cholesterol: 220mg

Slow Cooker Beef Barbacoa

SERVES 4
PREP TIME: 15 minutes
COOK TIME: 4 to 6 hours

DAIRY-FREE
GLUTEN-FREE
NUT-FREE
SOY-FREE

2 tablespoons Homemade Taco Seasoning (page 82)
1½ pounds chuck roast, cut into 2-inch cubes
¼ cup packed fresh cilantro
½ cup thinly sliced white onion
½ jalapeño pepper, finely minced, or 1 tablespoon chipotle peppers in adobo sauce (optional)
3 tablespoons freshly squeezed lime juice
2 tablespoons minced garlic
1 tablespoon apple cider vinegar
2 teaspoons salt
¼ teaspoon dried oregano

Barbacoa is a term frequently used in the present day to describe a method of slow-cooking meat until it's very tender. Barbacoa technique originates in Caribbean cuisine and is the source of the word "barbecue." Barbacoa preparations typically have a spicy, citrusy flavor profile. Try this barbacoa in Vegetarian Hummus Tacos (page 128), Southwest Breakfast Burritos (page 112), or any salad or grain bowl.

1. If needed, prepare the taco seasoning.

2. In a slow cooker, combine the chuck roast, cilantro, onion, jalapeño (if using), lime juice, garlic, taco seasoning, vinegar, salt, and oregano.

3. Cover the cooker and cook on High heat for 4 to 6 hours or on Low heat for 8 to 10 hours, or until the meat is cooked through and easily falls apart when prodded with a fork. Let cool until you can handle it, then shred the meat with 2 forks.

4. Evenly portion the barbacoa into one half of 4 large two-compartment glass meal-prep containers with tight-fitting lids. Fill the remaining compartment with a side or salad of your choice. Cover and refrigerate.

STORAGE: Keep refrigerated for up to 5 days. Reheat individual portions of barbacoa in the microwave on high power for 1½ to 2 minutes just before eating.

SUBSTITUTION TIP: If you don't eat beef, use the same amount of pork butt to make pork carnitas.

PER SERVING: Calories: 439; Total Fat: 30g; Saturated Fat: 12g; Protein: 34g; Total Carbohydrates: 7g; Fiber: 1g; Sugar: 1g; Cholesterol: 158mg

Sweet & Spicy Shrimp Bowl

SERVES 4
PREP TIME: 25 minutes
COOK TIME: 5 minutes

DAIRY-FREE
NUT-FREE
SOY-FREE

8 ounces dried
    soba noodles
1 cup warm water
½ cup sugar
¼ cup fish sauce
¼ cup freshly squeezed
    lime juice
2 tablespoons sambal
    oelek (red chile sauce)
2 tablespoons
    minced garlic
1 bell pepper, any color,
    julienned into ⅛-inch-
    thick strips
2 carrots, julienned into
    ⅛-inch-thick strips
1 red onion, julienned into
    ⅛-inch-thick strips
1 zucchini, spiralized or
    julienned into ⅛-inch-
    thick strips
¼ cup thinly sliced scallion,
    white and green parts
    separated
1½ pounds cooked shrimp,
    tails removed
¼ cup crushed cashews
    (optional)

If you're a big fan of seafood, you'll love this refreshing, flavor-packed sweet-and-spicy shrimp bowl. Enjoyed hot or cold (we prefer it cold), this dish features a combination of soba and zucchini noodles, with other fresh vegetables mixed in. Dressed in a tangy sweet and spicy sauce, it makes for a delicious work-week lunch or dinner.

1. Cook the soba noodles according to the package directions. Drain and set aside to cool.

2. Meanwhile, in a large bowl, whisk the warm water, sugar, fish sauce, lime juice, sambal oelek, and garlic until the sugar is dissolved.

3. Add the bell pepper, carrots, red onion, zucchini, scallion whites, and shrimp. Toss all ingredients to coat thoroughly.

4. Evenly portion the shrimp mixture into one half of 4 large two-compartment glass meal-prep containers with tight-fitting lids. Top with the scallion greens and cashews (if using). Evenly portion the soba noodles into the remaining compartment. Cover and refrigerate.

STORAGE: Keep refrigerated for up to 5 days. Just before eating, add the soba noodles to the shrimp mixture and stir to incorporate thoroughly. Enjoy cold or hot. To serve hot, reheat individual portions in the microwave on high power for 1½ to 2 minutes just before eating.

SUBSTITUTION TIP: If you're allergic to shellfish or you don't have shrimp on hand, replace the fish sauce with coconut aminos and replace the shrimp with diced cooked chicken.

PER SERVING: Calories: 446; Total Fat: 2g; Saturated Fat: <1g; Protein: 35g; Total Carbohydrates: 80g; Fiber: 3g; Sugar: 31g; Cholesterol: 270mg

Cilantro-Garlic Grilled Shrimp

SERVES 4
PREP TIME: 15 minutes
COOK TIME: 10 minutes

DAIRY-FREE
GLUTEN-FREE
NUT-FREE
SOY-FREE

3 garlic cloves, peeled
1 scallion, sliced, white and green parts
½ cup fresh parsley
½ cup fresh cilantro
2 tablespoons freshly squeezed lime juice
½ teaspoon minced peeled fresh ginger
½ teaspoon salt
¼ teaspoon freshly ground black pepper
⅛ teaspoon cayenne pepper (optional)
1 tablespoon avocado oil
1 pound large (21 to 25) raw shrimp, peeled and deveined

We love to grill shrimp on skewers over the weekend. Once prepped, add these bright, garlicky shrimp to lunch salads or wraps, or use them as a protein for quick and easy dinners. We recommend pairing the shrimp with Southwestern Bean & Corn Salad (page 41).

1. Preheat a grill to high heat. Soak 5 wooden skewers in water to prevent burning once grilled.

2. In the bowl of a food processor, combine the garlic, scallion, parsley, cilantro, lime juice, ginger, salt, black pepper, and cayenne (if using). Pulse on high speed in 30-second intervals until the mixture reaches a smooth consistency. With the food processor running, slowly drizzle in the oil. Set aside.

3. Slide 4 or 5 shrimp onto each soaked skewer. Skewer the shrimp through both the tail and the body, creating a "C" shape, to ensure even cooking. Brush the shrimp with half the cilantro sauce, reserving the other half for serving.

4. Gently lay the skewers on the grill and cook for 2 to 3 minutes. Flip the skewers and grill the shrimp on the other side for 1 to 2 minutes, until the shrimp are pink and opaque. Remove from the heat and take the shrimp off the skewers.

5. Portion 4 or 5 shrimp into one half of 4 large two-compartment glass meal-prep containers with tight-fitting lids. Top the shrimp with the reserved cilantro sauce. Fill the remaining compartment with a side or salad of your choice. Cover and refrigerate.

STORAGE: Keep refrigerated for up to 5 days. Reheat individual portions of shrimp in the microwave on high power for 1½ to 2 minutes just before eating.

INGREDIENT TIP: Switch up the sauces from prep to prep to keep the flavors fresh—we like to use pesto or any citrus marinade, such as our Zesty Lemon Vinaigrette (page 83).

PER SERVING: Calories: 110; Total Fat: 4g; Saturated Fat: <1g; Protein: 17g; Total Carbohydrates: 2g; Fiber: 1g; Sugar: <1g; Cholesterol: 150mg

Dill & Scallion Pesto–Baked Salmon

SERVES 4
PREP TIME: 15 minutes
COOK TIME: 25 minutes

GLUTEN-FREE

NUT-FREE

SOY-FREE

¼ cup extra-virgin olive oil,
  plus 1 teaspoon
1 cup fresh parsley leaves
¼ cup chopped scallions,
  white and green parts
1 tablespoon fresh dill
1 garlic clove, peeled
2 tablespoons freshly
  grated Parmesan
1 tablespoon freshly
  squeezed lemon juice
1 pound wild-caught
  salmon fillets, cut into
  4 pieces
½ teaspoon salt
¼ teaspoon freshly ground
  black pepper

This oven-baked salmon gets its bright, fresh flavor thanks to a homemade dill and scallion pesto. This easy recipe is highly customizable—swap out the greens in the pesto for other ingredients, such as basil, cilantro, and a bit of garlic. Pair the salmon with a whole grain, such as cooked brown rice or quinoa, and your favorite vegetable side and enjoy time and time again.

1. Preheat the oven to 350°F. Line a large baking sheet with foil and brush it with 1 teaspoon of oil. Set aside.

2. In the bowl of a food processor, combine the parsley, scallions, dill, garlic, Parmesan, and lemon juice. Pulse on high speed in 30-second intervals until the mixture reaches a smooth consistency. With the food processor running, slowly drizzle in the remaining ¼ cup of oil. Set the pesto aside.

3. Place the salmon fillets on the prepared baking sheet, skin side-down. Sprinkle the fillets with salt and pepper. Spread the dill pesto over each piece of salmon to cover it completely.

4. Place the baking sheet in the oven and bake for 20 to 25 minutes, or until the salmon reaches an internal temperature of 130°F (for medium) or 145°F (for well-done).

5. Place a salmon fillet in one half of 4 large two-compartment glass meal-prep containers with tight-fitting lids. Fill the remaining compartment with cooked brown rice or any side or salad of your choice. Cover and refrigerate.

STORAGE: Keep refrigerated for up to 5 days. Reheat individual portions in the microwave on high power for 1½ to 2 minutes just before eating.

COOKING TIP: This easy oven-baked method works with almost any type of hearty fish, including halibut, cod, and swordfish.

PER SERVING: Calories: 272; Total Fat: 19g; Saturated Fat: 4g; Protein: 24g; Total Carbohydrates: 2g; Fiber: 1g; Sugar: 2g; Cholesterol: 58mg

Measurement Conversions

VOLUME EQUIVALENTS	U.S. STANDARD	U.S. STANDARD (OUNCES)	METRIC (APPROXIMATE)
LIQUID	2 tablespoons	1 fl. oz.	30 mL
	¼ cup	2 fl. oz.	60 mL
	½ cup	4 fl. oz.	120 mL
	1 cup	8 fl. oz.	240 mL
	1½ cups	12 fl. oz.	355 mL
	2 cups or 1 pint	16 fl. oz.	475 mL
	4 cups or 1 quart	32 fl. oz.	1 L
	1 gallon	128 fl. oz.	4 L
DRY	⅛ teaspoon	–	0.5 mL
	¼ teaspoon	–	1 mL
	½ teaspoon	–	2 mL
	¾ teaspoon	–	4 mL
	1 teaspoon	–	5 mL
	1 tablespoon	–	15 mL
	¼ cup	–	59 mL
	⅓ cup	–	79 mL
	½ cup	–	118 mL
	⅔ cup	–	156 mL
	¾ cup	–	177 mL
	1 cup	–	235 mL
	2 cups or 1 pint	–	475 mL
	3 cups	–	700 mL
	4 cups or 1 quart	–	1 L
	½ gallon	–	2 L
	1 gallon	–	4 L

OVEN TEMPERATURES	
FAHRENHEIT	CELSIUS (APPROXIMATE)
250°F	120°C
300°F	150°C
325°F	165°C
350°F	180°C
375°F	190°C
400°F	200°C
425°F	220°C
450°F	230°C

WEIGHT EQUIVALENTS	
U.S. STANDARD	METRIC (APPROXIMATE)
½ ounce	15 g
1 ounce	30 g
2 ounces	60 g
4 ounces	115 g
8 ounces	225 g
12 ounces	340 g
16 ounces or 1 pound	455 g

Resources

WHAT'S IN SEASON PRODUCE GUIDE

As mentioned in part 1, if you're not sure what foods are in season when and where, we've created a complete guide that covers fresh produce options through winter, spring, summer, and fall. This guide will help you save money and tailor your meal preps to the seasons.

EmilyKyleNutrition.com/Seasonal-Produce-Guide

MEAL PREP KITCHEN EQUIPMENT AND CONTAINER GUIDE

Looking for a quick and easy shoppable post to stock up your kitchen? This guide is the one for you! We cover all the kitchen equipment, storage containers, and other products we use and recommend for meal prep.

EmilyKyleNutrition.com/Meal-Prep-Kitchen-Equipment-Guide

CLEAN EATING + CBD GUIDE

Many people wonder if CBD can be integrated into a clean-eating lifestyle. Speaking from the perspective of a certified Holistic Cannabis Practitioner, the answer is YES! I use CBD with my clients to help manage inflammation, along with many other health benefits—try the Anti-Inflammatory CBD Smoothie (page 94). If you're new to using CBD to support your health, consult this guide to help you get started.

EmilyKyleNutrition.com/Clean-Eating-CBD-Guide

EMILY KYLE NUTRITION

If you're ready to take your clean-eating meal-prep lifestyle one step further, visit our personal website for plenty of clean-eating and meal-prep BONUS content created specifically to accompany this book. You can also contact us there if you have any questions along your clean-eating journey.

EmilyKyleNutrition.com/Clean

BRITTNY HARRIS NUTRITION

Many people benefit from working one-on-one with a nutrition coach who can provide invaluable support in reaching your clean-eating and meal-prepping lifestyle goals. If you think this might be you, we'd love to recommend Brittny Harris, a Certified Transformational Nutrition Coach and trainer of badass women. She provides the guidance and accountability needed to make your new lifestyle change one that sticks.

BrittnyHarris.com

SHAW SIMPLE SWAPS

Another recommendation for one-on-one virtual nutrition coaching to help you reach your goals is Registered Dietitian Nutritionist, Certified Personal Trainer, and our good friend, Liz Shaw. Liz's specific specialties includes weight management, metabolic syndrome, high cholesterol, hypertension, cardiovascular health, and women's health, with an emphasis on fertility.

ShawSimpleSwaps.com

Index

About the Authors

EMILY AND PHIL KYLE are the husband-and-wife team behind Emily Kyle Nutrition (EKN).

Emily Kyle is an award-winning, nationally recognized media dietitian, nutrition spokesperson, speaker, three-time published author, and certified Holistic Cannabis Practitioner. Emily writes a nutrition and cannabis blog, where she shares evidence-based cannabis resources, nutrition articles, nutritious recipes, and her love of backyard gardening and modern homesteading.

Phil Kyle is an experienced chef and successful culinary entrepreneur with more than three decades of restaurant experience. After leaving his own restaurant in 2019, he has taken over the position of Executive Chef and Culinary Director for EKN.

By combining the knowledge of a dietitian and experience of a chef, EKN can develop high-quality recipes and stunning food photography for clients and brands alike. Emily and Phil now combine their talents to publish cookbooks including *The 30-Minute Thyroid Cookbook: 125 Healing Recipes for Hypothyroidism & Hashimoto's*, *The Hashimoto's AIP Cookbook: Easy Recipes for Thyroid Healing on the Paleo Autoimmune Protocol*, and *The Easy Thyroid Diet Plan, a 28-Day Meal Plan and 75+ Recipes for Symptom Relief.*

Outside of work, you can find Emily in her "she shed" and Phil on the farm caring for the gardens, flock of chickens, and their young son, Ransom. For more of their work, visit EmilyKyleNutrition.com.

CPSIA information can be obtained
at www.ICGtesting.com
Printed in the USA
JSHW011944130222
22790JS00007B/7